D1722234

little & friday

EVERY MEAL

PENGUIN BOOKS

PENGUIN

UK | USA | Canada | Ireland | Australia

India | New Zealand | South Africa | China

Penguin is an imprint of the Penguin Random House group of companies, whose addresses
can be found at global.penguinrandomhouse.com.

Penguin
Random House
New Zealand

First published by Penguin Random House New Zealand, 2016

1 3 5 7 9 10 8 6 4 2

Text © Kim Evans and Sophie Beck, 2016

Photography © Lottie Hedley, 2016

The moral right of the authors has been asserted.

All rights reserved. Without limiting the rights under copyright reserved above, no part
of this publication may be reproduced, stored in or introduced into a retrieval system, or
transmitted, in any form or by any means (electronic, mechanical, photocopying, recording
or otherwise), without the prior written permission of both the copyright owner and the
above publisher of this book.

Design by Holly McCauley © Penguin Random House New Zealand

Prepress by Image Centre Group

Printed and bound in China by RR Donnelley Asia Printing Solutions Ltd

A catalogue record for this book is available from the National Library of
New Zealand.

ISBN 978-0-14-357428-6

penguin.co.nz

———

———

It has been three years since the release of my last book, and so much has changed for us at Little & Friday in that time. We are no longer a small bakery, we have opened two new stores and we now employ 70 staff. This book is a reflection of where we are today and focuses on a more balanced way of eating and the need to accommodate people with special dietary requirements.

A huge topic in the food world at the moment is diets revolving around eliminating certain food groups – dairy, gluten, sugar. I believe that food isn't supposed to create stress or pressure. The best way to enjoy food is to focus on a healthy, balanced and nutritious diet, but don't allow yourself to feel guilty for also enjoying the occasional cream donut! Our cake cabinet is not 'every meal' food and our pie warmer isn't filled with 'every meal' food, so we decided to add to our offering the kind of food that can be enjoyed for every meal – salads for lunch and beautiful breakfasts cooked in our wood-fired oven.

A few years back the last little shop on our block in Belmont became available and we decided to provide our customers with the last meal of the day, dinner. It had previously been a quaint little roast shop, and over the years, as we worked late into the night rolling pastry and baking cakes, we watched as customers came by for their evening roast. We saw that many people on their way home from work don't have time to then turn around and spend 40 minutes in the kitchen in order to provide their family with a proper meal. So we opened After Hours as a test kitchen for the winter in 2014, offering fresh salads, wood-fired pizzas and a different home-style cooked meal every night of the week. Our same customers who came for their morning coffee and brioche would come back again at 7pm to pick up a hot meal with a slice of cheesecake for dessert.

The recipes in this book are a selection of the most popular meals on our menu, our favourite staff breakfasts and lunches, and the dinners that our After Hours customers begged for time and time again. This book, and the Little & Friday business, is now a collaboration between myself, a self-taught baker, and Sophie Beck, a professional chef. For the last four years we have been working together to make Little & Friday grow and evolve.

When I first started Little & Friday seven years ago – one tiny café initially open just one day a week – my ideal was to create an ethically correct food business. At first I thought that simply meant buying free-range animal products, recycling and supporting other small local suppliers. Each year reveals a deeper understanding of what it is to be ethically correct. For my business to be sustainable it's about a multi-dimensional way of operating. It's not just what we choose to purchase, but how I treat my staff and my community, the respect we have for the food, every choice we make to live harmoniously in our environment.

We've strived to build a community of suppliers that we feel proud to work with. To avoid leftover food going to waste, we deliver to the Auckland City Mission (they especially love the donuts). All of our food scraps are collected by Steve Rickerby of We Compost (see page 168). We were lucky to be one of Steve's first customers and we have watched his incredible business grow from one small truck to collecting 1500 kilograms of waste a week from all over Auckland. Over the years Steve has saved two million kilograms of waste from entering landfill.

We actively source from local produce suppliers with like-minded business principles. Transparency is so important, knowing where something came from and how it was produced. All Good Bananas provide us with the greatest spray-free organic bananas grown ethically in Ecuador. We get our honeycomb from Fred Jerschke (see page 16), who adores his bees (he calls them his girlfriends!) and produces the most sensational honey.

Running a food business this way can be a bumpy ride financially. My accountants over the years have often questioned my buying decisions. A battery-farmed egg costs 13 cents while a free-range egg costs 33 cents. When you are going through 10,000 eggs a week it makes quite a big difference. But my buying power is supporting another business trying to make decisions that aren't profit based. Otaika Valley Free Range Eggs supply us, and a growing number of food enterprises, which has meant they are now establishing a second farm to meet demand. Ours is not a highly profitable business model, but I am able to pay my bills and support a community of people working towards a positive environment.

My daughter Holly, who worked alongside me at the age of 15 starting Little & Friday, has now been able to start her own ceramic business, working from a little studio out the back of our Belmont premises and swapping plates and cups in return for rent. We've watched the people in our street and community start families, watched babies grow and seen many staff come through these doors and leave more skilled and wise.

Little & Friday has grown but our principles are still the same. To make good home-style food with produce from ethical sources, and ultimately to make our customers feel like they are entering our home for breakfast, lunch or dinner.

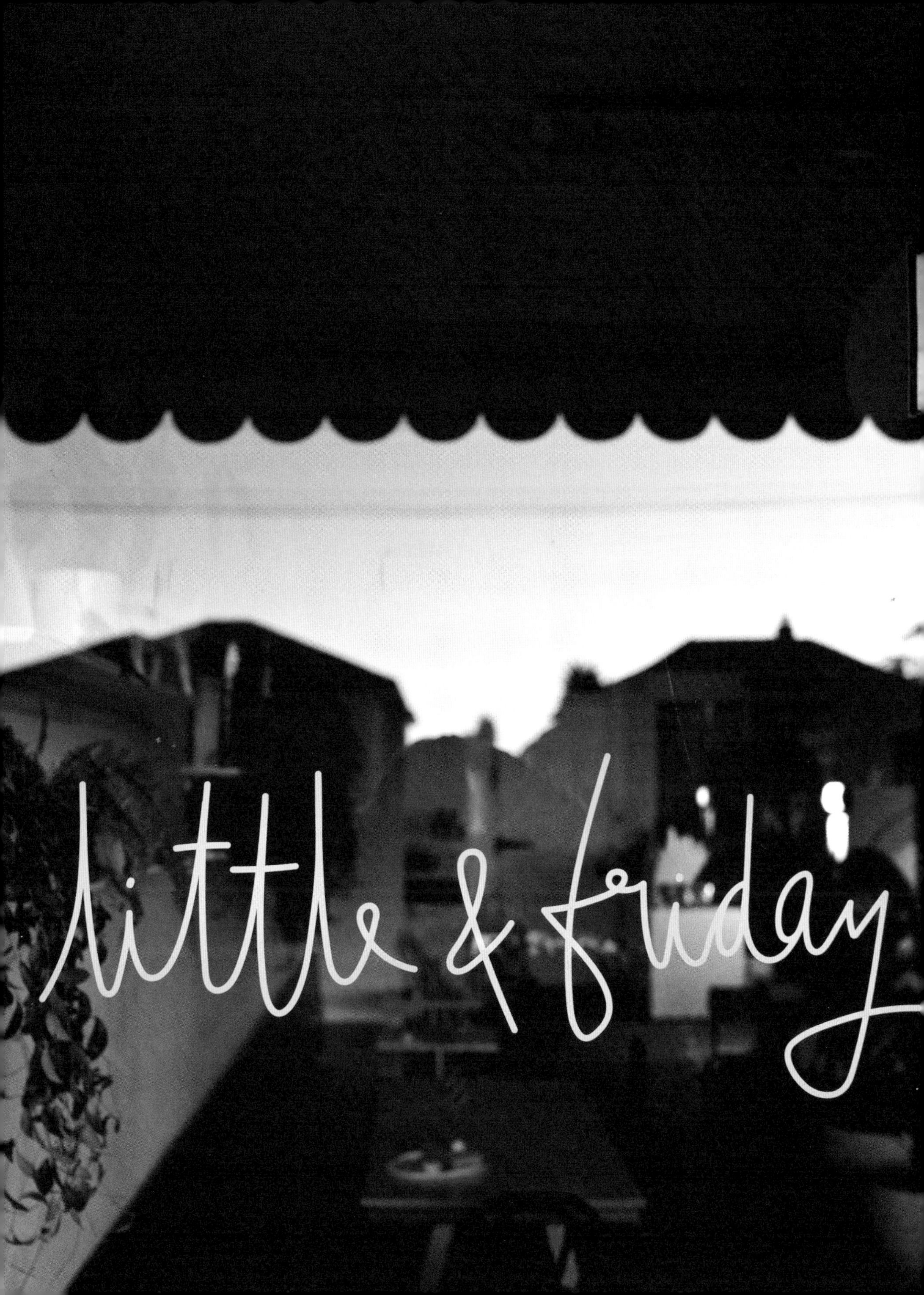
little & friday

BREAKFAST

—

We started out as a bakery and now through customer demand we have created a breakfast menu incorporating luscious baked goods, such as fig toast and crumpets, which you might make on a weekend morning, and muesli and porridge with a twist for a quick weekday breakfast.

In this section there is a recipe to fit every season. In summer we use loads of fresh fruits with our pancakes, brioche toast and muesli, and in winter, when fruit supplies become limited, we poach pears, apples and rhubarb, which are handy to have on hand in the fridge for breakfast or to top desserts. We endeavour to create delicious breakfast options for everybody, so now you will see gluten-free, dairy-free and sugar-free options included among our recipes, and the best thing is they are all easy!

MUESLI WITH COCONUT PANNA COTTA

—

THIS MUESLI HAS ALL THE GOODIES FOR A HEALTHY BREAKFAST. WE SERVE IT WITH A DELICIOUS, CREAMY DAIRY-FREE PANNA COTTA AND POACHED SEASONAL FRUIT. IT'S A GREAT WAY TO START THE DAY.

**MAKES 1KG MUESLI;
SERVES 6**

MUESLI
225g rolled oats
240g jumbo oats
45g puffed millet
85g sunflower seeds
85g pumpkin seeds
40g puffed amaranth
320g buckwheat
15g black sesame seeds
15g white sesame seeds
60g rice pops
390ml apple juice
125g honey
50ml oil (soy or coconut)

PANNA COTTA
2½ leaves gelatine
40g caster sugar
300ml coconut cream
75ml almond milk
250g coconut yoghurt
   (I use Raglan)

TO SERVE
1 recipe Poached Plums
   (see page 166)

—

Cook's note: Serve with extra
fresh or freeze-dried fruits and
top with edible flowers if desired.

—

TO MAKE THE MUESLI
1. Preheat oven to 150°C.

2. Mix dry ingredients in a large bowl until well combined.

3. Place apple juice, honey and oil in a small saucepan and boil for 1 minute.

4. Pour oil mixture over dry ingredients and mix until well combined.

5. Spread out over two baking trays and toast in oven for 40 minutes or until golden brown.

6. Allow to cool. If stored in an airtight container, it will keep for a month.

TO MAKE THE PANNA COTTA
1. Place gelatine leaves in a bowl of cold water for 10 minutes to soften.

2. In a small saucepan, combine sugar, coconut cream and almond milk. Stir over a low heat to dissolve sugar.

3. Remove gelatine from water and squeeze in your hands to remove excess water. Add gelatine to warm cream mixture and turn off heat. Keep stirring for a couple of minutes to ensure that the gelatine is fully mixed in. Pour panna cotta mix into a metal bowl.

4. Fill a larger bowl with ice and a little water to create an ice bath. Sit metal bowl over ice and keep stirring mixture until it just starts to thicken. Using a spatula, fold through the coconut yoghurt.

5. Pour panna cotta into a container and cover with a lid or cling film. Alternatively, you can divide the mix into individual ramekins. Allow to set in refrigerator for 3–4 hours, or overnight. The panna cotta should have a slight wobble.

TO SERVE
Divide muesli among individual serving bowls. Using a hot spoon, scoop panna cotta out and divide among bowls. If using individual ramekins, stand them briefly in hot water and then turn out onto muesli. Top with Poached Plums and serve with a jug of milk.

PORRIDGE WITH POACHED PEAR

—

SOPHIE CREATED THIS CREAMY PORRIDGE WHICH IS DAIRY-FREE AND HAS EXOTIC FLAVOURS. WE SERVE IT WITH A POACHED PEAR (SEE PAGE 166) AND SWEETENED WITH SOME OF FRED'S DELICIOUS HONEY. THE KEY TO A GOOD CREAMY PORRIDGE IS TO COOK IT LONG AND SLOW, A LITTLE LIKE A RISOTTO.

SERVES 6

1 vanilla bean
750ml coconut milk
750ml soy milk
5 whole cardamom pods,
    crushed
2 cups organic fine rolled
    oats
runny honey to taste

TO SERVE

1 recipe Poached Pears
    (see page 166)
chopped pistachio nuts
    (optional)
honeycomb or maple syrup
    (optional)

—

Cook's notes: For a thicker porridge, cook the oats for an extra couple of minutes. For a thinner porridge, add more coconut or soy milk.

For a fancier presentation, you can make the pears into fan shapes. Slice the bottom off the pear so it sits flat, core it, then slice around the outside every 3mm. Hold the stem at the top and twist.

—

1. Split vanilla bean in half and scrape out seeds. Reserve seeds and pod.

2. Place coconut milk, soy milk, cardamom pods and vanilla seeds and pod into a large saucepan. Heat to nearly boiling then turn down heat and simmer gently for 30 minutes.

3. Remove from heat and strain through a sieve into a bowl to remove vanilla and cardamom pods.

4. Return milk to pan and place over a low heat. Add oats and stir continuously until porridge starts to thicken (approximately 5–8 minutes). The oats should be soft to the taste (have no 'bite' to them) and the porridge should be a creamy consistency.

5. Add honey to taste.

6. Serve with a whole poached pear and a drizzle of the poaching syrup, scatter with chopped pistachios and serve honeycomb alongside or drizzle with maple syrup (if using).

HONEY SPICE PEAR LOAF

–

PEAR AND GINGER ARE A GREAT COMBINATION IN THIS LOAF WHICH WE MAKE WITH FRED'S HONEY.
IT IS DELICIOUS SERVED WITH BLUE CHEESE (WE USE MOERAKI) AND HONEYCOMB.

MAKES 1 LOAF

115g butter
1 cup firmly packed soft
   brown sugar
½ cup golden syrup
½ cup good-quality honey
2½ cups flour
2½ tsp baking powder
2 tsp ground ginger
1 tsp mixed spice
½ nutmeg, grated
2 tsp ground cinnamon
zest of 1 lemon
½ cup milk
1 beaten egg
½ cup ground almonds
3 Poached Pears
   (see page 166)
blue cheese, to serve
honeycomb, to serve

1. Preheat oven to 180°C. Grease a 23cm x 13cm loaf tin and line with baking paper.

2. Place butter, sugar, golden syrup and honey in a large saucepan. Heat gently, stirring with a wooden spoon until combined. When mixture is hot, remove from heat.

3. Sift flour, baking powder and spices into a large bowl. Add lemon zest.

4. Make a well in the centre of the dry ingredients and pour in the butter mixture. Stir well, then add milk and egg. Stir until fully combined. The mixture will be quite runny.

5. Place ground almonds in a separate bowl and roll the Poached Pears in almond until fully coated.

6. Pour loaf mixture into prepared tin. Push pears into mixture in an even row, leaving stalks protruding from the top.

7. Bake for 30 minutes. Reduce oven temperature to 170°C and turn loaf tin around in oven. Bake for another 40–50 minutes, until top of loaf bounces back when pressed.

8. Remove loaf from oven. Allow to cool, then remove from tin.

9. To serve, slice loaf thickly, toast in the oven for 5 minutes at 170°C and serve with blue cheese and honeycomb.

BREAKFAST CRUMPETS

—

CRUMPETS ARE TRICKY AND TAKE SOME PATIENCE AS THEY NEED TO BE COOKED ON A LOW HEAT – IT TAKES OUR CHEFS A GOOD FEW HOURS TO COOK THE 50 WE USE EACH DAY – BUT EXTRAS CAN BE KEPT IN THE FREEZER AND POPPED STRAIGHT INTO THE TOASTER WHILE FROZEN. IN WINTER YOU MAY NEED TO PROVE THE DOUGH IN A WARM PLACE, SUCH AS NEXT TO A HEATER OR IN A HOT WATER CUPBOARD.

SERVES 4

450ml warm milk
2½ tsp caster sugar
15g instant dry yeast
565g (4½ cups) high-grade
   flour
1 tsp salt
¾ tsp baking soda
350ml warm water
1–2 tbsp clarified butter (see
   Cook's note)

TO SERVE

1 recipe Caramelised
   Bananas (see opposite)
mascarpone
honeycomb
½ cup Candied Hazelnuts
   (see page 167)

—

Cook's note: If you use regular butter to cook these crumpets, the sugars in the milk solids will burn in the pan. To make your own clarified butter, cook butter very slowly on a low heat until milk solids drop to the bottom and clarified butter rises to the top. Skim the white foam off the surface, then pour off clarified butter into a lidded container, leaving the milk solids behind. Cool and refrigerate until needed.

—

1. Combine milk and sugar in the bowl of an electric mixer and sprinkle yeast over. Let stand for 2 minutes. The mixture should start to bubble.

2. Using a beater attachment, mix flour and salt into yeast mixture on medium speed until a soft dough forms.

3. Cover bowl with a tea towel and leave to prove at room temperature for 15–20 minutes (the tea towel will protect the dough from draughts that could affect the proving process).

4. Stir the baking soda into the warm water and pour into the bowl containing the dough mixture.

5. Return bowl to electric mixer and use a whisk attachment to beat, first on slow speed and then increasing to high speed as the mixture thickens. Continue beating until you have a smooth batter. This usually takes 10 minutes.

6. Cover bowl and leave to prove at room temperature until doubled in height (approximately 30 minutes, depending on the air temperature).

7. Melt 1 tablespoon of clarified butter in a frying pan over a low heat. Place three metal rings of approximately 8cm in diameter in pan, and pour ½ cup of mixture into each ring. Cook for 5 minutes. Sometimes a skin will form over the top of the crumpets as they are cooking and bubbles will struggle to come through. If this happens, carefully lift off the skin with a palette knife. Once bubbles have risen to the surface, place a square of tinfoil over the top of each ring for 30 seconds to set the crumpets.

8. Remove tinfoil and rings. Flip each crumpet and cook the other side until golden, approximately 2 minutes. Remove and allow to cool on a rack.

9. Toast crumpets, then serve 2 crumpets per person with Caramelised Bananas, a dollop of mascarpone, honeycomb and Candied Hazelnuts sprinkled over.

SEE PHOTO ON PAGE 22

CARAMELISED BANANAS

—

THESE CAN BE PREPARED WHILE YOUR CRUMPETS ARE COOKING. IF NECESSARY, COOK THEM
IN BATCHES AND KEEP WARM IN A PREHEATED OVEN.

SERVES 4

4 bananas, skin on
100g caster sugar
20g salted butter

—

Cook's note: If you want more
colour on the bananas, leave them
cut-side down in the pan for an
extra couple of minutes before
turning over.

—

1. Leaving skin on, halve each banana lengthways.

2. Place a frying pan large enough to hold all the bananas over
a medium heat. If pan is not large enough, cook in two batches.
Add sugar to pan and allow to caramelise. The sugar will turn an
amber colour.

3. Add bananas to pan, cut-side down, and cook for 3–4 minutes.
Add butter and cook for a further minute.

4. Remove pan from heat and turn bananas over so that they are
skin-side down. Spoon caramel from pan over bananas to coat.
Set aside until ready to use.

5. Serve 2 banana halves per person.

SEE PHOTO ON PAGE 22

BRIOCHE TOAST WITH AMARETTO APRICOTS

—

IF YOU AREN'T A FAN OF AMARETTO YOU COULD LEAVE IT OUT AND SPRINKLE OVER CHOPPED
TOASTED ALMONDS INSTEAD. THIS IS ALSO GOOD MADE WITH PLUMS OR PEACHES IN PLACE
OF THE APRICOTS.

SERVES 4

BRIOCHE LOAF
400g (2¾ cups) high-grade
   flour
2 tbsp caster sugar
pinch of salt
1 egg
2 egg yolks
150ml milk
40g fresh yeast
   (15g instant dry yeast)
120g unsalted butter,
   softened

EGG WASH
1 egg
1 tbsp cream

TO FINISH
8 apricots, halved
50g butter
¼ cup brown sugar
3 tbsp amaretto liqueur
¼ cup fresh blueberries
⅓ cup crème fraîche,
   to serve

TO MAKE THE BRIOCHE LOAF

1. Place flour, sugar, salt, egg and yolks, milk, yeast and 40g
of the butter in the bowl of an electric mixer with a dough hook
attachment. Mix on medium speed until fully combined.

2. Turn mixer to low speed, add another 40g of butter and mix
until fully combined. Repeat with the remaining 40g of butter and
mix until dough becomes smooth. This should take 15 minutes.

3. Mix on medium-high speed until dough comes together to form
a ball. Turn dough out onto a lightly floured bench.

4. Roll dough out to a rectangle measuring 30cm x 20cm. Fold the
two shorter ends into the centre, then fold in half lengthwise to
create a rectangle measuring 7.5cm x 20cm.

5. Lightly grease a 23cm x 13cm loaf tin. Pinch edges of dough together
and place in prepared loaf tin, pinched edges down. Cover with a tea towel
and leave to prove for 15–30 minutes, until it increases in size by half.

6. Preheat oven to 180°C.

7. To make egg wash, place egg and cream in a bowl and whisk until
smooth. Brush top of loaf with egg wash.

8. Using a sharp paring knife, score loaf by making three diagonal cuts
across the top about 2cm deep. Immediately place loaf in the centre of
the oven and bake for 10 minutes, then turn oven down to 160°C and
turn the loaf tin around. Bake for a further 10 minutes.

9. To check whether the brioche is cooked, tap the bottom: if it sounds
hollow, it is cooked. If not, bake for 5 minutes and test again, until
cooked. Remove from oven and allow to cool in tin.

TO FINISH

1. Place apricots in a baking dish. Add knobs of butter and scatter sugar
on top. Cook in oven for 10 minutes to soften. Sprinkle amaretto and fresh
blueberries over apricots and return to oven for 2–3 minutes.

2. Cut brioche into slices 2.5cm thick and toast in oven until golden.
Serve topped with apricots and blueberries, and dollops of crème fraîche.

FIG BREAD

—

THIS BREAD IS NOT CHEAP TO MAKE BUT IT KEEPS WELL AND IS SO FILLING YOU ONLY NEED ONE SLICE. WE SERVE IT WITH RASPBERRY AND FIG JAM MADE WITH FRESH FIGS HARVESTED FROM OUR GARDEN (SEE PAGE 171).

MAKES 1 LOAF

500g (3⅓ cups) high-grade
  flour
1 tsp salt
1 tsp honey
100g fresh yeast (30g
  instant dry yeast)
300ml lukewarm water
500g (3½ cups) whole dried
  figs, halved
150g (1½ cups) walnuts
70g (½ cup) currants
100g (¾ cup) dried apricots
50g (⅓ cup) mixed peel
½ tbsp ground cinnamon
½ tsp ground nutmeg
¼ tsp ground allspice
¼ tsp ground ginger

—

Cook's note: You need to use whole figs in this recipe, as pre-chopped figs will be too dry.

—

1. Mix together flour, salt, honey, yeast and 200ml water in an electric mixer using a dough hook on medium speed until elastic. Add more of the remaining water as required.

2. With the mixer on slow speed, add remaining ingredients until just mixed through. Don't over-mix.

3. Shape dough into a ball, place in a lightly greased bowl and cover with a tea towel. Leave for 30 minutes at room temperature to prove.

4. On a lightly floured bench, roll dough into a thick rectangle measuring 30cm x 20cm. Fold the two shorter sides in to join at the centre. Press the edges together along the top. It should now be a log shape.

5. Put dough into a proving basket with pinched edge on top, or place the loaf on a lightly floured baking tray between two lightly floured rolled tea towels to prevent loaf spreading. Cover with cling film and leave to prove for 1 hour at room temperature.

6. Preheat oven to 180°C. Line a baking tray with baking paper.

7. Place loaf on baking tray with pinched edge on the bottom. With a sharp knife, score a line 2cm deep down the length of the dough.

8. Pour boiling water into an oven dish and place it in the bottom of the oven. This will create steam for the beginning of the baking process. Turn oven down to 160°C and bake loaf for 30 minutes in the centre of the oven. After 30 minutes, turn baking tray around and cook for a further 20 minutes.

9. Tap base of loaf; a hollow noise means it is cooked. If it's not, bake for another 10 minutes and check again.

10. Allow to cool before slicing. This is delicious with home-made Raspberry and Fig Jam (see page 171) or Hazelnut Butter (see page 170).

BANANA BERRY TATIN

—

WE'VE INCLUDED THIS IN THE BREAKFAST SECTION BUT IT IS ANOTHER DECADENT DISH THAT COULD EASILY BE SERVED AS A DESSERT.

SERVES 6

200g caster sugar
50g butter
juice of 1 lemon
8 medium bananas
30cm-diameter circle of
    puff pastry 8mm thick
100g crème fraîche
1 punnet blueberries
¼ cup Candied Walnuts
    (see page 167)
2 tbsp runny honey, to serve
vanilla bean ice cream,
    to serve

1. Preheat oven to 180°C.

2. Place sugar in a large ovenproof frying pan, approximately 30cm in diameter. Cook over a moderate heat until sugar starts to melt and caramelise. Once sugar has reached a dark amber colour, add butter and lemon juice and turn heat off. Stir caramel until butter and lemon juice are incorporated.

3. Peel bananas and slice in half lengthways. Place banana slices cut-side down into hot caramel, and layer evenly around the pan. Top with the circle of puff pastry.

4. Bake in oven for around 30–35 minutes, until pastry is dark golden in colour.

5. Place a serving plate upside down over top of pan and flip tatin out. Be extremely careful not to spill caramel on yourself, as it will be very hot. The bananas should be on top, evenly layered across the pastry base.

6. Pour caramel juice from pan all over tatin. Dollop crème fraîche over the top, scatter with blueberries and walnuts and drizzle with honey to finish.

7. Serve immediately with a good-quality vanilla bean ice cream.

CHOCOLATE BRIOCHE

—

THIS IS A DELICIOUS WEEKEND BREAKFAST TREAT SERVED HOT STRAIGHT FROM THE OVEN.

MAKES 1 LOAF

FILLING
1 cup Chocolate Ganache
   (see page 164) or
   Hazelnut Spread (see
   page 150)
½ cup chocolate chips

DOUGH
400g (2¾ cups) high-grade
   flour
2 tbsp caster sugar
pinch of salt
1 egg
2 egg yolks
150ml milk
40g fresh yeast (15g instant
   dry yeast)
120g unsalted butter,
   softened

EGG WASH
1 egg
1 tbsp cream

icing sugar, to dust

1. Make Chocolate Ganache (see page 164) or Hazelnut Spread (see page 150). Set aside.

2. Place flour, sugar, salt, egg and yolks, milk, yeast and 40g of the butter in the bowl of an electric mixer with a dough hook attachment. Mix on medium speed until fully combined.

3. Turn mixer to low speed, add another 40g of the butter and mix until fully combined. Repeat with the remaining 40g of butter and continue mixing until dough becomes smooth. This should take 15 minutes in total.

4. Mix on medium-high speed until dough comes together to form a ball. Turn dough out onto a lightly floured bench.

5. Mix filling ingredients in a bowl until fully combined.

6. Roll out dough to a rectangle about 30cm x 20cm. Spread filling over dough, then roll up into a log. Cut log in half lengthways, then twist the separate lengths together to form one loaf, overlapping left to right. Pinch the ends closed.

7. Lightly grease a 23cm x 13cm loaf tin. Place dough in prepared loaf tin with pinched ends folded to the bottom. Cover with a tea towel and leave to prove for 15 minutes.

8. Preheat oven to 160°C.

9. To make egg wash, place egg and cream in a bowl and whisk until smooth. Brush top of loaf with egg wash.

10. Place loaf in the centre of the oven. Bake for 15 minutes, then turn loaf tin around and turn oven down to 150°C. Bake for a further 15 minutes.

11. To check whether the brioche is cooked, tap the bottom: if it sounds hollow, it is cooked. If not, bake for 5 minutes and test again, until cooked. Remove from oven and leave to cool in tin before turning out. Dust with icing sugar.

KIM'S BRAN MUFFINS

—

I STARTED MAKING BRAN MUFFINS IN MY TEENS MANY MOONS AGO. THIS IS ONE OF MY ORIGINAL RECIPES WHICH HAS STOOD THE TEST OF TIME. HONEY IS USED IN PLACE OF SUGAR SO THEY MAKE A REALLY HEALTHY BREAKFAST ON THE RUN. WE LIKE TO SERVE THEM WITH WHIPPED BUTTER (SEE PAGE 170).

MAKES 12

1 cup chopped dates
½ cup water
4 tbsp good-quality honey
1¼ cups flour
pinch of salt
2 tsp baking powder
1 tsp ground ginger
1 tsp ground cinnamon
1 cup bran flakes
1 egg
3 tbsp coconut oil
¾ cup coconut milk
1 banana, mashed
1 cup walnut pieces

GARNISH

1 banana, thinly sliced
4 tbsp demerara sugar
(optional)

1. Preheat oven to 180°C. Grease and line 12 muffin tins with baking paper.

2. Place dates, water and honey in a small saucepan and cook over a medium heat until a soft paste forms, approximately 10 minutes. Allow to cool slightly.

3. Sieve flour, salt, baking powder and spices into a large bowl. Add bran flakes and mix to combine.

4. In a separate bowl, lightly whisk egg and oil together, then stir through coconut milk, mashed banana and walnuts, and finally the date paste.

5. Gently fold banana mixture into dry ingredients until combined.

6. Divide mixture evenly between muffin tins. Top each muffin with 2 slices of banana and a sprinkling of demerara sugar (if using).

7. Bake in centre of oven for 25 minutes. Turn out onto a wire rack to cool.

FRUIT CUSTARD BRIOCHES

—

THESE BRIOCHES CAN BE MADE WITH ALL KINDS OF SEASONAL POACHED FRUITS. WE USE PLUMS, APRICOTS AND RHUBARB.

MAKES 6

DOUGH
400g (2¾ cups) high-grade
    flour
2 tbsp caster sugar
pinch of salt
1 egg
2 egg yolks
150ml milk
40g fresh yeast
    (15g instant dry yeast)
120g unsalted butter,
    softened

FILLING
1 recipe Frangipane
    (see page 161)
1 recipe Crème Pâtissière
    (see page 160)
1 recipe (12) Poached Plums
    (see page 166)

EGG WASH
1 egg
1 tbsp cream

icing sugar, to dust
1 tbsp freeze-dried
    raspberries, to serve

1. Place flour, sugar, salt, egg and yolks, milk, yeast and 40g of the butter in the bowl of an electric mixer with a dough hook attachment. Mix on medium speed until fully combined.

2. Turn mixer to low speed and add another 40g of butter and mix until fully combined. Repeat with the final 40g of butter and continue mixing until dough becomes smooth. This should take 15 minutes in total.

3. Mix on medium-high speed until dough comes together to form a smooth ball.

4. Place dough in a greased bowl, cover with a tea towel and leave at room temperature to prove. This will take 20–30 minutes depending on the weather; the dough should about double in size.

5. Preheat oven to 160°C.

6. Roll dough out on a lightly floured bench to a thickness of 2cm.

7. Use a cookie cutter to cut out circles 6cm in diameter. Use the base of a cup or glass about 1cm smaller than the dough circles to press down on the circles to form a cavity.

8. Put 1 tablespoon Frangipane into each cavity. Put 2 tablespoons Crème Pâtissière over Frangipane and top with 2 Poached Plums.

9. Leave to prove for 15 minutes.

10. To make egg wash, place egg and cream in a bowl and whisk until smooth. Brush egg wash over dough.

11. Place brioches in oven and bake for 20 minutes or until golden. Remove from oven, dust with icing sugar and sprinkle with freeze-dried raspberries to serve.

BACON AND EGG STUFFED AVOCADO

—

THIS IS A SUPER EASY DISH THAT IS DAIRY-FREE AND GLUTEN-FREE AND GOOD IF YOU HAVE
A BIG GROUP COMING FOR BRUNCH. WE LIKE TO SMASH THE AVOCADO SALAD ONTO TOAST
AND EAT IT WITH THE BAKED EGGS.

SERVES 6

6 Hass avocados
juice of 3 limes
12 slices free-range smoked
    middle bacon
12 large eggs
salt and freshly ground
    black pepper
3 tbsp good-quality extra
    virgin olive oil
1 bunch coriander, roughly
    chopped

1. Preheat oven to 200°C.

2. Halve avocados and scoop out flesh into a bowl; don't scrape
too close to the skin. Dress avocado with lime juice and allow
to marinate for 10–15 minutes.

3. Line each avocado half with a rasher of bacon. The bacon
should come up 2–3 centimetres above the skin of the avocado.
This ensures that the egg won't spill out.

4. Crack an egg into each avocado half.

5. Season with salt and freshly ground black pepper. Place in an
ovenproof dish and bake for 13–15 minutes. The egg yolk will still
be runny when eaten – cook longer if you want firmer eggs.

6. Add olive oil, coriander, salt and freshly ground black pepper to
the bowl of lime-dressed avocado. Toss gently and check seasoning.

7. Once eggs are cooked, serve 2 avocado halves per person with
the lime, coriander and avocado salad.

COCONUT BREAD WITH MANGO SALSA

—

FOR A QUICK SUMMERY BREAKFAST YOU CAN FREEZE SLICES OF THIS LOAF SO IT'S ALWAYS ON HAND WHEN YOU FANCY SOMETHING A LITTLE MORE DELICIOUS THAN YOUR NORMAL BREAKFAST.

SERVES 6

COCONUT BREAD
2 eggs
300ml milk
1 tsp vanilla paste
2½ cups flour
2 tsp baking powder
1 cup caster sugar
2 cups shredded coconut
75g unsalted butter, melted
3 medium bananas, mashed

PANNA COTTA
3 leaves gelatine
150ml cream
225ml milk
80g caster sugar
½ tsp vanilla paste
pulp of 2 passionfruit,
    to serve

MANGO SALSA
2 mangoes, cut into 1cm
    cubes
pulp of 2 passionfruit
¼ cup ripped mint leaves
juice of 1 lime

TO MAKE THE COCONUT BREAD

1. Preheat oven to 180°C. Grease a 23cm x 13cm loaf tin and line with baking paper.

2. Whisk eggs, milk and vanilla until combined.

3. In a separate bowl, combine flour, baking powder, sugar and coconut.

4. Make a well in the centre of the dry ingredients and gently stir in milk mixture.

5. Stir in melted butter and bananas to just combine. Do not over-mix, or the loaf will be tough.

6. Pour mixture into prepared loaf tin and place in the centre of the oven. Bake for 50–60 minutes, turning tin around after 30 minutes. The loaf is ready when the top bounces back when pressed.

TO MAKE THE PANNA COTTA

1. Place gelatine leaves in a bowl of cold water for 10 minutes to soften.

2. Put cream, milk, sugar and vanilla in a saucepan and bring to a gentle simmer, stirring to dissolve the sugar. Do not let it boil. Remove from heat.

3. Remove gelatine from water and squeeze to remove excess water, then place in hot milk mixture and stir to dissolve.

4. Divide equally between six ramekins and place in the refrigerator overnight or for at least 6 hours, to set.

TO MAKE THE MANGO SALSA
Combine all ingredients in a bowl.

TO SERVE
Spoon passionfruit pulp over panna cotta to garnish. Serve with slices of coconut bread topped with mango salsa.

BLUEBERRY PANCAKES

—

THESE PANCAKES CAN BE MADE WITHOUT SUGAR. THE HONEY BUTTER IS SWEET ENOUGH
FOR ANYONE GOING REFINED SUGAR-FREE.

SERVES 6

POACHED BLUEBERRIES
1 cup frozen blueberries
1 tbsp unsalted butter
½ tsp vanilla paste

HONEY BUTTER
100g honeycomb
250g Whipped Butter (see
  page 170)

PANCAKES
50g butter for frying
4 eggs, separated
1 cup fresh ricotta
¾ cup full-cream milk
50g butter, melted
1 cup flour
1 tsp baking powder
pinch of salt
zest of 1 orange
¼ cup caster sugar
  (optional)

TO MAKE THE POACHED BLUEBERRIES
Place blueberries, butter and vanilla in a saucepan over a low
heat and gently simmer for 5 minutes. Remove from heat.

TO MAKE THE HONEY BUTTER
Fold honeycomb through whipped butter until just combined.

TO MAKE THE PANCAKES
1. Clarify the butter for frying the pancakes – melt it and then let
it sit until it separates. Use the runny yellow layer on top to cook
with (this won't burn as you cook the pancakes).

2. Place egg whites in a clean, dry, stainless-steel bowl. In another
bowl, combine egg yolks, ricotta, milk and melted butter.

3. Sieve flour, baking powder and salt into a third bowl and stir in
orange zest and sugar, if using. Create a well in the centre of the
dry ingredients and slowly pour the ricotta mixture in, then gently
fold to combine.

4. Whisk egg whites until they form stiff peaks.

5. In two separate lots, fold egg whites through the mixture until
just combined. Finally, fold through half the poached blueberries.
Do not over-mix.

6. Heat a frying pan over a medium heat. Grease 3 egg rings and
place on base of pan.

7. Scoop a third of a cup of pancake mixture into each ring and
cook until bubbles appear on the surface.

8. Remove rings and flip pancakes. Cook for a further minute
or two until lightly golden.

9. Serve 3 pancakes stacked on each plate with the remaining
poached blueberries spooned over and honey butter on the side.

POTATO RÖSTI WITH ROCKET PESTO

—

IT'S REALLY IMPORTANT TO USE AGRIA POTATOES FOR THIS RECIPE AS THEY GIVE THE RÖSTI A FLUFFY TEXTURE AND GOLDEN, CRISPY CRUST. THIS IS A REALLY GOOD HANGOVER BREAKFAST!

SERVES 4

RÖSTI
1.5kg Agria potatoes, peeled
1 tbsp good-quality Dijon
    mustard
salt and freshly ground
    black pepper
2 tbsp olive oil

ROCKET PESTO
50g walnuts, whole or
    pieces
50g grated Parmesan
100ml good-quality extra
    virgin olive oil
150g rocket leaves
½ clove garlic
juice of ½ lemon

TO FINISH
350g free-range streaky
    bacon
1 tbsp runny honey
8 free-range eggs
2 ripe Hass avocados
2 handfuls of rocket leaves
juice of 1 lemon
2 tbsp good-quality extra
    virgin olive oil

1. Place potatoes in a large saucepan, cover with cold water and add a good pinch of salt. Bring to the boil, then reduce heat and cook gently for 5–8 minutes. Drain and allow to cool. Grate coarsely. Mix grated potato with mustard, salt and pepper.

2. Line a 20cm x 20cm cake tin with baking paper. Press potato firmly into tin. Place in refrigerator for at least 2 hours (or overnight) to set.

3. Preheat oven to 180°C. Put an oven tray in oven to preheat.

4. Turn the square of grated potato out onto a board and cut into 4 pieces.

5. Remove tray from oven and drizzle with oil. Place potato squares on tray and drizzle with a little more oil. Bake for 35–40 minutes, turning over halfway through. Rösti should be a nice golden colour on both sides and crispy on the outside.

6. To prepare pesto, lightly toast walnuts in a frying pan for a few minutes, stirring regularly to avoid burning. Allow to cool slightly.

7. Place all pesto ingredients in a blender and whizz on high speed until smooth and a vibrant green colour. Check and adjust seasoning if necessary.

8. Place bacon in an oven dish and drizzle with honey. Bake until golden and crispy.

9. Carefully place eggs in boiling water and cook for 5½ minutes. Drain eggs and place in iced water to cool. When cool enough to handle, gently peel.

10. Halve avocados, remove stones and scoop flesh out into a bowl. Add rocket, lemon juice and olive oil and gently toss together. Season with a little salt and freshly ground black pepper.

11. Place a rösti on each plate. Top with 2 soft-boiled eggs, slightly cracking each egg so that the yolk starts to run out. Season with salt and freshly ground black pepper.

12. Divide avocado and rocket salad between plates. Finish by topping each dish with honey-roasted bacon and dollops of rocket pesto.

Quite often I will skip lunch as I am too busy to stop and eat, so I will start the day with a really good breakfast and then hang out until dinner. But lunch doesn't need to be complicated. We aim for three clean flavours and no fuss, but the quality of the ingredients used in each dish is paramount.

In New Zealand we are lucky to be surrounded by amazing produce. These recipes make the most of this abundance thanks to the many clever artisan producers now supplying cafés and stores, such as the Clevedon Valley Buffalo Company, which makes authentic mozzarella, and Curious Croppers, whose heirloom tomatoes are just like the ones my grandmother used to grow.

You'll find recipes for summer salads packed with flavour, and for winter we have included a belly-warming soup and a classic sausage roll – so good for a lazy Sunday lunch around the fire.

PUMPKIN AND BARLEY SOUP

—

THIS IS ONE OF OUR MOST POPULAR SOUPS IN THE CAFÉ. IT IS SUPER HEARTY, THICK AND NOURISHING.

SERVES 6

1 cup pearl barley
2 buttercup pumpkins
   (approximately 1.5kg
   each)
salt and freshly ground
   black pepper
pinch of dried chilli flakes
100ml extra virgin olive oil
2 cinnamon sticks
½ bunch celery, including
   leaves, finely chopped
2 red onions, finely diced
handful of sage leaves,
   finely chopped
3 cloves garlic, minced
3cm piece fresh ginger,
   peeled and finely grated
1.5 litres chicken or
   vegetable stock
100g crème fraîche, to serve
50g shaved Parmesan,
   to serve
crusty bread, to serve

1. Cover pearl barley with cold water and leave to soak overnight, then drain.

2. Preheat oven to 200°C. Line an oven tray with baking paper.

3. Peel pumpkins, scoop seeds out and cut flesh into rough chunks. Season with salt, freshly ground black pepper and chilli and toss together with half the olive oil and the cinnamon sticks. Tip onto prepared tray and bake for 15–20 minutes or until pumpkin is cooked and golden. Remove from oven and allow to cool.

4. Gently heat remaining oil in a large saucepan or stockpot. Add celery, red onion and sage and cook for 8–10 minutes on a low heat. Add salt and freshly ground black pepper, garlic and ginger. Cook for a further 5 minutes.

5. Add everything from the roasting pan to the pot and mix together. The pumpkin should start breaking down into the celery mix.

6. Pour in stock and pearl barley. Bring to a simmer. Cook on a very low heat (do not boil) for 40–45 minutes or until barley is cooked. Stir occasionally to stop soup from catching on the bottom.

7. Depending on how thick or thin you like your soup, feel free to add more stock to create the desired consistency. Check for seasoning and adjust if necessary.

8. Remove cinnamon sticks before serving. Finish with a dollop of crème fraîche and a sprinkle of shaved Parmesan, and serve with crusty bread.

CHARRED SWEETCORN SALAD

—

THIS IS ONE OF OUR MOST POPULAR SUMMER SALADS AND IS ALSO GREAT SERVED WITH
BARBECUED MEATS. THE JALAPEÑO IS OPTIONAL SO LEAVE IT OUT IF YOU ARE SCARED OF 'HOT'.

SERVES 6

500ml olive oil
400g good-quality canned
    butter beans or chickpeas,
    rinsed and drained
pinch of sea salt
4 cobs sweetcorn, husk on
2 avocados
juice of 2 limes
2 whole pickled jalapeño
    peppers, sliced thinly
    (optional)
1 handful of coriander,
    including stalks, roughly
    chopped
2 red onions, finely chopped
100ml good-quality extra
    virgin olive oil
salt and freshly ground
    black pepper

—

Cook's note: To cook your own
chickpeas, place 500g dried chickpeas
in a large bowl, cover with water and
soak overnight. Drain chickpeas and
place in a large saucepan. Add water
to just cover and a couple of sprigs of
sage, 2–3 tomatoes, 2 celery stalks,
½ garlic bulb and 3 tbsp extra virgin
olive oil. Bring to the boil then reduce
heat and simmer uncovered for
1½–2 hours. (You may need to skim
off any foam that forms on the
surface.) Drain any remaining water,
remove the veges and season with
salt and freshly ground pepper.

—

1. For frying the butter beans or chickpeas, you will need a pan
large enough to allow the beans or chickpeas to sit in a single layer,
or cook in batches. Pour oil into pan and place over a medium heat.

2. Once oil starts to just smoke, carefully tip in beans or chickpeas.
Fry until golden in colour – this takes approximately 8–10 minutes.
Remove beans or chickpeas from oil with a slotted spoon and put
on paper towels to drain off excess oil. Season with sea salt and
allow to cool.

3. Cook sweetcorn cobs in a large pot of boiling salted water, with
husks on, for 12 minutes. Remove from water and allow to cool.

4. Once cobs are cool, strip husks off and either barbecue or grill
the whole cobs until all kernels turn a dark golden colour.

5. Slice corn kernels off the cob and place in a bowl. For variation,
you can cut the kernels off two cobs and cut the other two cobs
into thick slices.

6. Cut avocados in half, remove stone and skin and cut flesh
into chunks. Add to the bowl with the corn.

7. Add lime juice, sliced jalapeño (if using), beans or chickpeas,
coriander, red onion and olive oil.

8. Lightly toss together and season to taste with salt and freshly
ground black pepper. Serve straight away after dressing.

MUSHROOMS WITH SPICED CHICKPEAS

—

THIS IS A GLUTEN-FREE VEGETARIAN OPTION PACKED WITH FLAVOUR. THE STUFFED MUSHROOMS
CAN BE SERVED AS A LIGHT MEAL OR AS PART OF A MAIN MEAL.

SERVES 4

2 tbsp olive oil, plus extra
    for drizzling
2 red capsicums, deseeded
    and finely diced
2 carrots, peeled and finely diced
1 red onion, finely diced
salt and freshly ground
    black pepper
1 clove garlic, finely chopped
400g canned chickpeas,
    rinsed and drained
pinch of dried chilli flakes
1 tsp ground coriander
1 tsp ground cumin
1 tsp ground sumac
handful of roughly chopped
    coriander, stalks and leaves
3 handfuls of baby spinach
100g haloumi, grated
8 large portobello mushrooms

BASIL YOGHURT PESTO
30g pine nuts, plus extra for
    garnish (see below)
2 handfuls of basil leaves
⅓ cup grated Parmesan
100ml good-quality extra
    virgin olive oil
juice of ½ lemon
½ clove garlic
150ml thick unsweetened
    Greek-style yoghurt
salt and freshly ground
    black pepper

GARNISH
20g toasted pine nuts
handful of basil leaves

1. In a medium saucepan, heat oil over a moderate heat. Add capsicum, carrot, onion and salt and freshly ground black pepper and reduce heat to low. Cook for 15–20 minutes or until vegetables are soft but not brown. Add garlic and cook for 2–3 minutes.

2. Add chickpeas and spices and cook for a further 30 minutes on a low heat. You want the chickpeas to start to soften and smash up a little bit, but most to stay whole. Check seasoning and adjust if necessary, and remove from heat. Allow to cool.

3. Preheat oven to 180°C. Line a baking tray with baking paper.

4. Fold chopped coriander, baby spinach and grated haloumi through cooled chickpea mix.

5. Place mushrooms cap-side down on prepared tray. Season with a little salt and freshly ground black pepper.

6. Divide chickpea mix over mushrooms. Pile into centre of each mushroom, leaving a 1cm gap around the edge, as the mix spreads slightly during baking.

7. Drizzle with a little olive oil and bake for 15–20 minutes.

8. Lightly toast pine nuts by dry-roasting them in a frying pan for a few minutes, stirring regularly to avoid burning. Allow to cool. Set aside some for garnish.

9. Place all pesto ingredients in a blender and whizz on high speed until you have a smooth consistency and a vibrant green colour. Check seasoning and adjust if necessary.

10. Transfer mushrooms to a serving platter and dollop pesto over the top. Garnish with toasted pine nuts and fresh basil. Serve 2 stuffed mushrooms per person.

ASIAN SLAW

—

SOPHIE COUNTS THIS SALAD AS HER FAVOURITE OF ALL TIME. IT'S WORTH SOURCING THAI BASIL
AS IT REALLY ADDS TO THE ASIAN FLAVOUR.

SERVES 6

SALAD

1½–2 cups raw peanuts,
　skins removed
½ red cabbage
1 mango, peeled
300g sugar snaps or
　snow peas
1 cup Thai basil leaves
1 cup coriander leaves
1 cup roughly chopped mint
　leaves
500g packet (2 cups)
　mung bean sprouts

DRESSING

juice of 2 limes
2½ tbsp white sugar
½ cup warm water
¼ cup fish sauce
¼ cup rice wine vinegar
2 cloves garlic, minced
　or finely grated
1 chilli, deseeded and
　finely chopped

1. Lightly toast peanuts by dry-roasting them in a frying pan for
a few minutes, stirring regularly to avoid burning. Allow to cool
slightly, then roughly chop.

2. Thinly slice cabbage and mango. Trim sugar snaps or snow peas,
leaving them whole.

3. Toss all salad ingredients together, being careful not to over-mix
or crush any ingredients.

4. To make the dressing, combine lime juice and sugar, mixing until
dissolved. Add remaining dressing ingredients and mix to combine.

5. Toss dressing through salad mix and serve immediately. If not
eating straight away, dress just before serving.

FENNEL AND LEMON PASTA SALAD

—

FENNEL WAS NOT AROUND IN NEW ZEALAND WHEN I WAS GROWING UP. IT'S A POPULAR VEGETABLE IN ITALIAN CUISINE THANKS TO ITS ANISEEDY FLAVOUR AND GREAT CRUNCH. FORTUNATELY IT'S NOW AVAILABLE YEAR ROUND AND IS PERFECT IN THIS LEMONY PASTA SALAD.

SERVES 6

500g dried farfalle
400g crème fraîche
100ml good-quality extra
    virgin olive oil
100g grated Parmesan
zest and juice of 3 lemons
salt and freshly ground
    black pepper
150g rocket leaves, roughly
    chopped
2 fennel bulbs, thinly sliced

—

Cook's note: Can be made 4–5
hours ahead of time.

—

1. In boiling salted water, cook the farfalle for 10–12 minutes or until al dente, then rinse the pasta in cold water and set aside.

2. In a bowl, mix together crème fraîche, olive oil, Parmesan, lemon zest and juice. Season with salt and freshly ground black pepper.

3. Add cooked pasta, rocket and fennel to the bowl and toss together until just mixed.

4. Check seasoning and serve.

UDON NOODLES WITH GINGER SOY BROTH

—

THIS IS A GREAT VEGETARIAN OPTION. YOU CAN ALSO USE THE BROTH TO ADD DUMPLINGS TO.

SERVES 4

BROTH
2 cloves garlic
4 shallots
2 parsnips
2 red kumara
2cm piece ginger, skin on
1 medium broccoli head
2 carrots
½ bunch celery
1 bunch coriander
1 red chilli
3 litres water
300ml good-quality
    soy sauce
⅓ cup kecap manis (dark
    sticky soy sauce)
500g fresh udon noodles

GARNISH
4 spring onions, thinly sliced
    on an angle
1 red chilli, thinly sliced
coriander tops from broth
    ingredients
2 tsp black sesame seeds
2 tbsp sesame oil

—

Cook's note: Add vegetables
of your choice to the strained
broth, if desired.

—

1. Peel garlic, shallots, parsnips and kumara and chop roughly. Place in a large stockpot (with a 5- to 6-litre capacity).

2. Roughly chop ginger, broccoli, carrots and celery, including celery leaves. Add to stockpot.

3. Cut stalks and roots off coriander and wash. Reserve coriander leaves for garnish. Deseed chilli and chop roughly. Add coriander and chilli to stockpot.

4. Add remaining broth ingredients except udon noodles to stockpot. Bring to the boil and then turn right down so it is lightly simmering.

5. Allow to gently simmer for 1 hour. Check seasoning, and add extra soy sauce and kecap manis if needed (rather than salt).

6. Using either a muslin cloth laid over a colander or a fine sieve, strain vegetables from broth. Pour broth back into pot and heat gently. Add udon noodles and cook for 4–5 minutes.

7. For the garnish, toss together spring onion, chilli slices, coriander leaves and black sesame seeds.

8. Divide udon noodles among 4 bowls and pour broth over each. Serve with garnish on top and a drizzling of sesame oil.

KALE AND PARSNIP SALAD

—

WE ARE NOT BIG ON MIXING FRUIT WITH SAVOURY INGREDIENTS BUT THIS REALLY WORKS. BLOOD
ORANGES ARE AVAILABLE THROUGH AUTUMN AND THEY MAKE FOR A SALAD WITH A DIFFERENCE.

SERVES 6

2kg parsnips, skin on
150ml maple syrup
50ml olive oil
salt and freshly ground
    black pepper
200g sliced almonds,
    plus extra for garnish
    (see below)
500g kale, washed
5–6 blood oranges
150g shaved Parmesan
    (optional)

DRESSING
juice of 1 orange
25ml maple syrup
80ml good-quality olive oil
1 tbsp sherry vinegar
salt and freshly ground
    black pepper

TO GARNISH
50g toasted sliced almonds
50g shaved Parmesan
    (optional)

—

Cook's note: I recommend dressing
the salad just before serving it.
You can use navel oranges if you
cannot get blood oranges.

—

1. Preheat oven to 180°C. Line an oven tray with baking paper.

2. Trim ends of parsnips and cut lengthways into quarters. Toss
in a bowl with maple syrup, oil, salt and freshly ground black
pepper. Place on prepared tray and bake for 15–20 minutes or
until golden and tender. Remove from oven and allow to cool.

3. Lightly toast sliced almonds by dry-roasting them in a frying
pan for a few minutes, stirring regularly to avoid burning. Allow
to cool slightly. Set aside quantity needed for garnish.

4. Strip kale from stalks and chop roughly. Place in bowl large
enough to toss all salad ingredients in.

5. Peel oranges and cut into 1cm slices. Add to bowl of kale along
with toasted almonds, Parmesan (if using) and roasted parsnip.

6. In a separate bowl, combine dressing ingredients. Add to salad
and gently toss together.

7. Serve on a large platter, scattered with extra toasted almonds
and shaved Parmesan (if using).

ROAST VEGE SALAD

—

RADICCHIO GIVES THIS SALAD A REAL TASTE HIT WITH ITS BITTER BITE AND ALSO ADDS A SHOT OF COLOUR. AS THIS IS A SIMPLE SALAD IT IS IMPORTANT TO USE THE BEST QUALITY INGREDIENTS YOU CAN AFFORD. I LIKE TO USE AN AGED BALSAMIC VINEGAR FROM GIUSEPPE GIUSTI.

SERVES 6

500g baby carrots
1kg fennel bulbs
500g baby orange kumara
salt and freshly ground
    black pepper
50ml olive oil
1 large radicchio
25ml good-quality aged
    balsamic vinegar
50ml good-quality extra
    virgin olive oil

1. Preheat oven to 180°C. Line a large oven tray with baking paper.

2. Trim baby carrots, leaving an inch of green above the top of each carrot, and place in a large bowl.

3. Trim stalks off fennel bulbs and remove outer layer of fennel. Cut into wedges about the same size as the baby carrots (approximately 6 wedges out of 1 fennel bulb). Add to bowl.

4. Cut baby orange kumara in half, or into pieces about the same size as the baby carrots. Add to bowl.

5. Toss all the cut vegetables with salt and freshly ground black pepper and olive oil. Place in a single layer on prepared oven tray. Bake for 15–20 minutes or until veges are nice and golden and a knife goes through them easily. Remove from oven and allow to cool.

6. Using the tip of a sharp knife, cut around root of radicchio and pull it out. Tear radicchio into 4 pieces, ripping through the layers.

7. In a large bowl, gently toss together roasted vegetables and radicchio with aged balsamic vinegar. Drizzle with extra virgin olive oil. Check seasoning and adjust if necessary.

8. Serve on a large platter alongside your favourite roasted meat.

TOMATO AND MOZZARELLA BRUSCHETTA

—

THIS RECIPE IS A REAL CROWD PLEASER. WE GO OUT OF OUR WAY TO FIND THE BEST TOMATOES AND LIKE TO USE THE LOCAL CLEVEDON VALLEY BUFFALO MOZZARELLA. MUSHING THE GARLIC AND TOMATOES INTO THE TOASTED CIABATTA IS THE KEY TO MAKING THIS BRUSCHETTA TASTE REALLY GREAT.

SERVES 4

1 loaf good-quality ciabatta
1 tbsp olive oil
1 clove garlic, peeled
1kg mixed heirloom tomatoes
    or good-quality vine
    tomatoes
3 tbsp good-quality sherry
    vinegar
salt and freshly ground
    black pepper
150ml good-quality extra
    virgin olive oil
500g fresh buffalo
    mozzarella (2 x 125g
    balls)
handful of fresh oregano
    leaves

–

Cook's note: As this recipe is quite simple and only includes a few ingredients, it is really important that you use the best quality you can find. Look for oxheart, Spanish green, black or yellow heirloom tomatoes to make a real impact.

–

1. Preheat oven to 160°C. Line a baking tray with baking paper.

2. Slice whole loaf of ciabatta in half lengthways. Place cut-side up on prepared tray. Drizzle with 1 tablespoon of olive oil and place in oven for 10–12 minutes, or until golden and crisp. You want to really dry out the bread as much as you can.

3. Once ciabatta is well toasted, remove from oven and rub generously with garlic clove.

4. Cut tomatoes into thick slices. Using your fingertips, push tomato slices into the toasted ciabatta, leaving some whole pieces and some smashed. Really push tomato into toast so that it doesn't just sit on top, but is mashed into the bread.

5. Splash all over with sherry vinegar and season with salt and freshly ground black pepper. Drizzle over half the extra virgin olive oil.

6. Tear mozzarella into bite-sized pieces and divide between the pieces of ciabatta. Scatter with oregano leaves and finish by drizzling remaining olive oil over mozzarella.

7. Cut ciabatta pieces in half and divide between 4 plates. Serve immediately.

LAMB AND FETA PITA POCKETS

—

THESE MAKE A GREAT SUMMER MEAL WHICH KIDS LOVE. WE SERVE 2 PITA POCKETS PER PERSON, BUT ANY LEFTOVERS ARE DELICIOUS FOR LUNCH THE NEXT DAY.

SERVES 5

5 Pita Breads (see opposite)

LAMB
¼ cup Onion Jam (see page 171)
375g lamb mince
1 clove garlic, minced
½ carrot, finely grated
½ red chilli, deseeded and
    finely chopped
2 tsp ground coriander
2 tsp ground cumin
100g feta, broken into chunks
1 tbsp roughly chopped mint leaves
salt and freshly ground
    black pepper

SALAD
½ red onion, sliced thinly
handful of Italian parsley
handful of mint leaves, chopped
handful of coriander, chopped
½ tbsp thinly sliced preserved
    lemon
juice of ½ lemon
½ tbsp good-quality extra
    virgin olive oil
salt and freshly ground
    black pepper

YOGHURT DRESSING
250g thick unsweetened
    Greek-style yoghurt
½ clove garlic, minced
juice and zest of 1 lemon
salt and freshly ground black
    pepper
25ml good-quality extra
    virgin olive oil
pinch of ground cinnamon

1. Make Pita Breads following recipe opposite.

2. Make Onion Jam following recipe on page 171. Leave to cool.

3. Soak 20 wooden skewers in water. Preheat barbecue until hot, or preheat oven to 200°C.

4. Gently combine Onion Jam with remaining lamb ingredients, making sure you can still see chunks of feta (don't over-mix).

5. Shape into 5 sausage-sized logs and thread onto wet wooden skewers.

6. Grill on hot barbecue, turning often until cooked. Alternatively, drizzle logs with olive oil and cook in oven for 8–10 minutes until cooked through. Lower the temperature of the oven to 180°C.

7. Toss salad ingredients together.

8. Combine yoghurt dressing ingredients.

9. Warm pita pockets in the oven and cut each in half.

10. Remove meat sausages from skewers. Cut in half and place 2 pieces in each pita pocket. Add a handful of salad and top with a dollop of yoghurt dressing. Serve immediately.

SEE PHOTO ON PAGE 76

PITA BREADS

—

THIS RECIPE MAKES MORE BREADS THAN YOU NEED FOR THE LAMB AND FETA PITA POCKETS (SEE OPPOSITE), BUT THESE FREEZE WELL AND ARE ALWAYS HANDY TO HAVE ON HAND FOR LUNCHES OR A QUICK AND EASY MEAL.

MAKES 10 PITA BREADS

750g (5 cups) high-grade flour
2 tsp salt
15g fresh yeast (5g instant
   dry yeast)
1½–1¾ cups lukewarm water

1. Using an electric mixer with a dough hook attachment, combine all ingredients and mix until elastic. Take a small piece of dough and start to pull the corners out with your fingers to create a 'window' with the dough. When it is ready, you should be able to see light through it without it breaking.

2. Shape dough into a ball and place in a greased bowl. Cover with cling film and leave to stand at room temperature for 1 hour.

3. Preheat oven to 220°C and place a baking tray in oven to preheat. Line a second baking tray with baking paper.

4. After standing dough, turn it out onto a lightly floured bench, cut into 10 even-sized pieces and roll each piece into a ball. Place dough balls on the lined baking tray, cover with a tea towel and leave to prove for 10 minutes.

5. On a lightly floured bench, roll out each ball to a flat circle 1cm thick. Cover with the tea towel and leave for another 10 minutes to prove.

6. Turn oven down to 200°C. Remove hot tray and place dough circles on the tray. Bake for 3 minutes. They will puff up halfway through, but keep them in the oven for the full time to cook the middles.

7. Remove from oven and allow to cool on racks.

SEE PHOTO ON PAGE 77

SAUSAGE ROLLS

—

THESE ARE A STAPLE ON OUR MENU. IF YOU DON'T EAT PORK, SUBSTITUTE FREE-RANGE CHICKEN MINCE OR CHICKEN SAUSAGE MEAT. YOU COULD ALSO USE CHICKEN SAUSAGES AND REMOVE THE MEAT FROM THE CASINGS.

MAKES 6

FILLING
2 tsp fennel seeds
¾ cup shelled pistachio nuts
1kg free-range pork sausage
    meat
½ cup grated Parmesan
4 tbsp apple or pear chutney
¼ cup finely chopped
    fresh sage
salt and freshly ground
    black pepper, to taste

EGG WASH
1 egg
1 tbsp cream

PASTRY
1 recipe Flaky Pastry
    (see page 158)

GARNISH (OPTIONAL)
6 sage leaves

1. Preheat oven to 200°C. Line a baking tray with baking paper.

2. Lightly toast fennel seeds by dry-roasting them in a frying pan for a few minutes, stirring regularly to avoid burning. Allow to cool, then grind with a mortar and pestle or in a spice grinder.

3. Lightly toast pistachio nuts in a frying pan for a few minutes, stirring regularly to avoid burning. Allow to cool, then chop roughly.

4. Gently combine filling ingredients. Fry a small amount of the filling mixture, then taste and adjust seasoning if necessary.

5. Lightly whisk eggs and cream together to make egg wash.

6. Cut the 30cm x 40cm pastry sheet in half lengthways, to make two long rectangular strips measuring 15cm x 40cm.

7. Lay one pastry strip across a lightly floured bench with the long side towards you, and shape half the filling mixture into a sausage along the middle of the pastry. Paint a line of egg wash along one side and roll the pastry to tightly enclose the filling. Repeat with the other sheet of pastry and remaining filling.

8. Cut each log into three even-sized pieces and put sausage rolls, seam-side down, on the prepared baking tray.

9. Score tops of sausage rolls twice with a sharp knife, brush with egg wash and decorate with a single sage leaf if desired.

10. Bake for 20–25 minutes until golden brown.

DINNER

–

These are our top picks from our dinner shop, After Hours, and are heavily influenced by Sophie's extensive travels through Asia. We utilise cuts of meats that you might not use normally, but which are ideal for slow methods of cooking, especially if you seal your cooking pot using the flour and water method described on page 100. It becomes a home-made pressure cooker – a little messy, but the result is worth the clean-up.

Sophie has converted us to an alternative way of cooking – the mighty wood-fired oven. If you ever get the chance to add one to your home, we highly recommend it. It is an exciting way of cooking as you need to be present; it's not about pressing a button and walking away. When entertaining guests, they will gather around the oven as it creates quite a theatrical atmosphere. We play around with using different woods to alter and develop flavours, whether roasting or smoking. Roasting large cuts of meat slowly overnight in the embers results in that mouth-watering charcoal flavour. It's great for making quick pizzas, too.

SPICED THAI PORK MEATBALLS

—

THIS IS A SUPER FRESH SUMMER MEAL. THE MEATBALLS ARE BEST MADE THE DAY BEFORE TO ALLOW THE FLAVOURS TO DEVELOP. FOR AN ALTERNATIVE, REPLACE THE MEATBALLS BY PAN-FRYING TOFU AND ADDING IT TO THE SALAD.

SERVES 6

MEATBALLS
1kg pork mince
½ carrot, finely grated
4 tbsp fish sauce
3 tsp sugar
6 coriander stalks, finely chopped
4 cloves garlic, minced
1 shallot, finely diced
salt and freshly ground
    black pepper
juice of 1 lime
3 tbsp peanut oil, for cooking

SALAD
250g dried vermicelli
1 iceberg lettuce, shredded
450g packet blanched shelled
    edamame beans
1 cucumber, sliced into
    matchsticks
handful of roughly chopped mint
handful of roughly chopped
    coriander
handful of roughly chopped
    Thai basil

NUOC CHAM DRESSING
2 cloves garlic, minced
1 chilli, deseeded and chopped
½ carrot, finely grated
¼ cup water
¼ cup fish sauce
¼ cup rice vinegar
2½ tbsp caster sugar

TO SERVE
150g peanuts, roughly chopped
3 limes, halved

TO MAKE THE MEATBALLS
1. Combine all meatball ingredients except oil and roll into 30 bite-sized balls.

2. Heat oil in a frying pan and cook meatballs in batches (taking care not to overcrowd them), turning to brown them all over (approximately 5–8 minutes). Remove meatballs from the pan and set aside. Keep warm.

3. Place lime halves in pan cut-side down to caramelise.

TO MAKE THE SALAD
1. Place vermicelli in a bowl and cover with boiling water. Leave for 10 minutes until cooked. Drain.

2. Combine all dressing ingredients.

3. Toss together all salad ingredients until well combined.

TO SERVE
1. Lightly toast peanuts by dry-roasting them in a frying pan for a few minutes, stirring regularly to avoid burning. Allow to cool slightly.

2. Divide salad among 6 bowls. Top with 5 meatballs per bowl and drizzle with dressing. Serve with half a caramelised lime each and toasted peanuts.

SCALLOPS WITH LEMON POTATOES

—

THE POTATOES ARE ALMOST THE STAR OF THIS DISH. FOR THE BEST FLAVOUR MAKE SURE THE
LEMONS REALLY CARAMELISE WHEN COOKING WITH THE POTATOES. YOU COULD SERVE THE
POTATOES WITH ANY SEAFOOD OR CHICKEN.

SERVES 4

POTATOES
2kg Agria potatoes
2 lemons
2 handfuls of oregano leaves
3 cloves garlic, finely
    chopped
75ml good-quality extra
    virgin olive oil
salt and freshly ground
    black pepper

SCALLOPS
8 rosemary stalks
32 fresh scallops
salt and freshly ground
    black pepper
olive oil, for brushing
1 lemon cut into 4 wedges,
    to serve

1. Preheat oven to 200°C. Line a roasting pan with baking paper.

2. Peel potatoes and cut into slices roughly 1cm thick. Quarter lemons and remove seeds, then slice thinly across each lemon quarter.

3. Put all ingredients for potatoes into prepared roasting pan. Using your hands, mix everything together well. Spread potato out evenly and cover pan with tinfoil. Roast in oven for 40 minutes.

4. Take pan out and remove tinfoil. Give potatoes a quick stir and put back into oven uncovered. Cook for a further 20–25 minutes until potatoes and lemon are golden.

5. If using a barbecue to cook the scallops, preheat it 20 minutes before you are ready to cook: you want the hotplate or grill to be as hot as you can get it. Alternatively, the scallops can be cooked in a hot frying pan in the same way. (It is not necessary to oil the pan as the scallops are brushed with oil.)

6. Trim rosemary stalks to a length that will allow 4 scallops to fit easily on each one. Leaving a few rosemary leaves at the end of each stalk, remove all other sprigs to make room for the scallops.

7. Pierce 4 scallops onto each stalk. Season with salt and freshly ground black pepper and brush a little oil over each scallop to prevent them from sticking to the barbecue or frying pan.

8. Grill skewers for 3–4 minutes on each side.

9. Divide potatoes among 4 plates, and place 2 skewers on each plate. Serve immediately with a wedge of lemon on the side.

LINGUINE WITH LEMON PANGRATTATO

—

YOU CAN MAKE THE TOMATO SAUCE IN ADVANCE AND FREEZE IT FOR A SUPER QUICK MEAL. AND THE PANGRATTATO IS DELICIOUS SERVED ON ANY PASTA DISH FOR A NICE CRUNCH AND EXTRA FLAVOUR.

SERVES 4

TOMATO AND BALSAMIC SAUCE
50ml good-quality extra virgin olive oil
3 cloves garlic, thinly sliced lengthways
handful of fresh basil leaves
5 red capsicums, finely diced
salt and freshly ground black pepper
100ml good-quality aged balsamic vinegar
4 x 400g cans whole or chopped organic tomatoes, drained

LEMON PANGRATTATO
500ml olive oil
1 clove garlic
2 cups day-old white breadcrumbs
salt
zest of 2 lemons
½ cup roughly chopped Italian flat-leaf parsley

TO FINISH
500g dried linguine
50g butter
extra virgin olive oil, to serve
roughly chopped Italian parsley, to serve

TO MAKE THE TOMATO SAUCE
1. Heat oil in a large saucepan over a low heat. Gently fry sliced garlic until it just starts to colour.

2. Add basil, capsicum, salt and freshly ground black pepper, and stir. Cook gently until capsicum is soft, approximately 15 minutes.

3. Add vinegar and tomatoes and cook on a low heat for 45–50 minutes until reduced to a thick sauce.

TO MAKE THE LEMON PANGRATTATO
1. While sauce is cooking, heat olive oil in a separate saucepan over a low heat. Gently fry garlic clove until golden, then remove.

2. Slowly add breadcrumbs to oil and cook until golden, stirring occasionally to prevent burning.

3. Remove from heat, drain carefully and spread breadcrumbs on paper towels to absorb excess oil. Season with salt.

4. Place breadcrumbs in a bowl and mix through lemon zest and parsley.

TO FINISH
1. Bring a large saucepan of salted water to the boil and cook linguine according to packet instructions until it is al dente. Drain, reserving 1 cup of cooking water.

2. Pour linguine into a large serving bowl and fold through the tomato sauce and butter, adding reserved cooking water, a little at a time, to achieve your desired consistency (the sauce should be quite wet). Check seasoning and adjust if necessary.

3. Divide among plates. Sprinkle generously with olive oil, parsley and pangrattato and serve immediately.

POTATO GNOCCHI WITH SAGE BUTTER

—

GNOCCHI IS ONE OF THOSE DISHES THAT GETS BETTER THE MORE YOU PRACTICE MAKING IT. THE KEY IS NOT TO OVER-MIX THE POTATOES AND FLOUR; IT'S FINE IF SOME OF THE FLOUR HAS NOT BEEN FULLY INCORPORATED. YOU CAN MAKE THIS RECIPE ALL YEAR ROUND AND JUST CHANGE WHAT YOU SERVE IT WITH. IN SPRING, NEW SEASON PEAS, GOAT CHEESE AND MINT ARE A FAVOURITE.

SERVES 4

1.5kg Agria potatoes, washed
flaky sea salt
300g pasta flour (tipo 00),
    plus extra if necessary
200g fine semolina
1 tbsp olive oil
250g exotic mushrooms,
    such as oyster, enoki,
    shiitake
salt and freshly ground
    black pepper
handful of sage leaves
1 clove garlic, finely chopped
150g unsalted butter
100g grated Parmesan
1 tbsp good-quality extra
    virgin olive oil

1. Place potatoes in a large saucepan and cover with cold water. Add a good handful of flaky salt. Bring to the boil, then reduce heat and simmer until potatoes are cooked – when done, a knife should pass easily through them.

2. Drain potatoes and allow to cool to the point where you can peel them with your hands. Do not let them go cold.

3. Once peeled, use a fork to gently mash the potatoes onto the bench. You want to keep them nice and fluffy. Don't worry if there are a couple of lumps; the main goal is to keep the potatoes aerated and light.

4. Season potatoes with salt and scatter with pasta flour. Ever so gently, fold potato together with flour. Stop folding when it is just mixed. There will still be bits of flour not quite incorporated.

5. Bring a small saucepan of water to the boil to test gnocchi dough.

6. Cut gnocchi dough into quarters. Roll one quarter into a thin log about 2.5cm in diameter and cut log into bite-sized pieces.

7. Test gnocchi dough by adding a couple of pieces to the boiling water. Once they float back to the top, take them out and check seasoning. If they start to fall apart in the water, the dough needs more flour. Gently fold a couple of handfuls of extra flour into the dough, along with extra seasoning if necessary. Test again in the boiling water.

8. When gnocchi pieces are the right consistency, roll and cut remaining dough as before.

9. Dust a tray with a couple of handfuls of semolina and transfer all the gnocchi onto it. Toss gnocchi in semolina to coat. The gnocchi will keep for several hours at room temperature before cooking, if necessary.

10. When ready to cook the gnocchi, add 1 tbsp olive oil to a hot frying pan. Add mushrooms and salt and freshly ground black pepper. Fry for a couple of minutes on a high heat. Add sage leaves and garlic, and fry for a further 2–3 minutes. Add butter and reduce heat to low. Mushrooms should be soft and glossy. Remove from heat, check seasoning and adjust if necessary.

11. Bring a large saucepan of water to the boil. Add a good handful of salt, and all the gnocchi. Once gnocchi start floating to the top (they take about 3–4 minutes to cook), remove them from the water and place straight into the pan of mushrooms. Toss together gently.

12. Divide among 4 plates. Sprinkle with grated Parmesan and a drizzle of extra virgin olive oil.

SEE PHOTO ON PAGE 93

CHICKEN MARYLAND WITH CAVOLO NERO

—

CAVOLO NERO IS SUCH AN UNDER-RATED VEGETABLE. IT'S A FANTASTIC WINTER GREEN THAT CAN BE USED IN PLACE OF SPINACH AND IS DELICIOUS CHOPPED AND ADDED TO SOUPS AND STEWS.

SERVES 6

FILLING
500g mascarpone
100g shredded Parmesan
⅓ cup finely chopped thyme
1 clove garlic, finely chopped
zest and juice of 1 lemon
salt and freshly ground
    black pepper
1 cup fresh breadcrumbs

CHICKEN
6 free-range chicken
    Marylands, skin on
    (200–250g each)
salt and freshly ground
    black pepper

BRAISED CAVOLO NERO
2kg cavolo nero
2 tbsp good-quality extra
    virgin olive oil
2 cloves garlic, finely sliced
1 tsp ground fennel seed
pinch of dried chilli flakes
salt and freshly ground
    black pepper

1. Preheat oven to 170°C. Line an oven dish with baking paper.

2. Place all filling ingredients in a bowl and mix until well combined. Check seasoning and adjust if necessary.

3. With your fingers, carefully separate the skin from the flesh of the chicken. This is to make room for the filling to go under the skin. Be careful not to tear the skin.

4. Using your hands, gently spread filling under the skin on each piece of chicken. Try not to get too much filling on top of the skin.

5. Place chicken in prepared oven dish and season with salt and freshly ground black pepper. Cook in oven for 35–40 minutes, or until chicken juices run clear. Remove from oven and leave to rest for 15 minutes before serving.

6. Bring a large saucepan of salted water to the boil.

7. Strip stalks from cavolo nero. Once water is boiling, add all the cavolo nero and cook for 8–10 minutes, or until it is soft.

8. Tip cavolo nero into a colander to drain. Transfer onto a clean, dry tea towel and give it a gentle squeeze.

9. Heat olive oil in a large saucepan or frying pan over a medium heat. Add garlic and cook for 2–3 minutes. As soon as garlic starts to turn golden, add fennel seed and chilli flakes. Cook for a further 1 minute.

10. Add cooked cavolo nero, salt and freshly ground black pepper. Keep cooking on a medium heat for 8–10 minutes, stirring frequently. Check seasoning and adjust if necessary, then remove from heat.

11. Transfer cavolo nero to a serving dish. Place chicken pieces on top and pour over any cooking juices.

SMOKED FISH PIE

—

THIS WAS A POPULAR DISH IN OUR BELMONT DINNER SHOP AFTER HOURS AND IS A GOOD DISH
TO MAKE THE DAY BEFORE. YOU COULD USE OTHER FISH SUCH AS SMOKED KAHAWAI AND GURNARD
IF YOU ARE NOT A FAN OF SALMON.

SERVES 8-10

FILLING
50g butter
50ml good-quality olive oil
4 large leeks, roughly
   chopped
1 cauliflower, stem trimmed,
   halved then sliced thickly
salt and freshly ground
   black pepper
2 cups fresh or frozen peas
zest of 4 lemons
2 tbsp roughly chopped fresh
   basil
2 tbsp roughly chopped fresh
   Italian parsley
2 whole fillets (approx. 1kg)
   of hot-smoked salmon
800g crème fraîche

TOPPING
2kg orange kumara, peeled
2 tbsp flaky sea salt
2 tbsp maple syrup

1. Preheat oven to 200°C.

2. Place butter and oil in a saucepan over a low heat. Add leek, cauliflower, salt and freshly ground black pepper. Cook gently until tender, 10–15 minutes.

3. Remove from heat. Add peas, lemon zest, basil and parsley. Gently combine.

4. Break salmon into flakes and fold into vegetables along with the crème fraîche, mixing until just combined. Check seasoning and adjust if necessary.

5. Chop kumara into chunks and place in a large saucepan. Cover with cold water and add flaky sea salt. Bring to the boil, then reduce heat and simmer until a knife passes easily through kumara (approximately 15 minutes).

6. Drain kumara and leave in the colander for 5 minutes, then mash until smooth. Season with salt and freshly ground black pepper to taste.

7. Place filling in a large ovenproof dish. Cover with kumara mash.

8. Brush mash with maple syrup and cook in oven for 35–40 minutes, until top is golden.

9. Serve hot with a wedge of lemon and a green salad or steamed greens.

BEEF PIE WITH SMASHED CELERIAC TOPPING

—

AT LITTLE & FRIDAY AFTER HOURS, WE WOULD COOK THIS IN OUR WOOD-FIRED OVEN OVERNIGHT, SEALED IN THE POT USING A 50/50 FLOUR-AND-WATER DOUGH. YOU COULD DO THIS IN A CONVENTIONAL OVEN AT 100°C. JUST BE WARNED IT DOES MAKE QUITE A MESS!

SERVES 4

FILLING
1kg beef shin
2 tbsp flour
salt and freshly ground
    black pepper
2 tbsp olive oil
1 bunch celery, trimmed
2 red onions
300g free-range smoked
    streaky bacon
2 tbsp finely chopped thyme
3 cloves garlic, finely
    chopped
750ml good-quality red wine
    (I use Shiraz)
750ml beef stock

TOPPING
1.5kg celeriac, peeled
3 cloves garlic, peeled
sea salt and freshly ground
    black pepper
50g butter
100ml good-quality olive oil,
    plus extra for drizzling
100g shredded Parmesan

1. Preheat oven to 160°C.

2. Dice beef shin into bite-sized pieces. Season flour with salt and freshly ground black pepper.

3. Put oil in a large, lidded ovenproof pot that can be used on the stovetop, and heat over a high heat.

4. Lightly dust beef pieces in seasoned flour before adding to oil. Fry over a medium to high heat until all pieces are golden brown. Remove beef from pot.

5. Chop celery finely and add to pot. Roughly dice onions, cut bacon into 2cm pieces and add to pot with chopped thyme. Cook over a medium heat for 15–20 minutes, or until celery is soft and bacon slightly golden. Add chopped garlic and cook for a further 2 minutes over a low heat.

6. Add meat back to pot, and pour over wine and stock. Season with a little salt and freshly ground black pepper and place lid on pot. Transfer to the oven. Cook for 2½ hours or until meat is tender and pie filling has a thick consistency. Remove from oven, check seasoning and adjust if necessary.

7. Cut celeriac into large chunks. Place celeriac and garlic in a saucepan and add water to just cover. Add a good pinch of sea salt. Bring to the boil, reduce heat and simmer for approximately 20–25 minutes until tender.

8. Drain celeriac in a colander and return to the pan. Add butter and oil, and roughly mash celeriac with a potato masher or a solid whisk, retaining some chunky pieces. Season to taste.

9. Divide filling among 4 ovenproof pie dishes or large ramekins. Top each with smashed celeriac, drizzle with a little extra olive oil and sprinkle with Parmesan.

10. Increase oven temperature to 180°C. Bake for 20 minutes or until celeriac topping is golden and crusty. Serve hot.

SLOW-ROASTED LAMB SHOULDER

—

THIS IS SOPHIE'S ALL-TIME FAVOURITE ROAST LAMB RECIPE. THE JUICES MAKE A BEAUTIFUL, SWEET GRAVY AND LEFTOVER LAMB IS GREAT THE NEXT DAY SERVED IN WRAPS AND SANDWICHES WITH FRESH MINT, YOGHURT AND WATERCRESS.

SERVES 6

3 red onions
2 whole bulbs garlic
1 whole lamb shoulder on
    the bone (2–2.5kg)
5 sprigs rosemary
2 tbsp olive oil
salt and freshly ground
    black pepper
1 litre cranberry juice
new season baby potatoes,
    to serve
mint sprigs, to serve

1. Preheat oven to 200°C.

2. Cut red onions into large pieces and scatter over the base of a large roasting dish, big enough to hold the lamb shoulder. Cut garlic bulbs in half horizontally and add to dish.

3. Place lamb shoulder bone-side down on top of onion. Add sprigs of rosemary. Drizzle lamb with oil and season with salt and freshly ground black pepper.

4. Roast in oven for 25–30 minutes, or until lamb is nice and golden. Turn oven down to 140°C and add cranberry juice to dish.

5. Cook for a further 2 hours, basting every 30 minutes with the cooking juices.

6. When ready, remove lamb from oven and allow to rest for 30 minutes before carving. Serve with new season baby potatoes and fresh mint.

STUFFED CHICKEN WITH EGGPLANT SALAD

–

THE STUFFING USED IN THIS CHICKEN IS A GOOD OPTION FOR GLUTEN-INTOLERANT EATERS.
WE LIKE TO SERVE THE EGGPLANT SALAD WARM BUT IT IS JUST AS DELICIOUS SERVED AT
ROOM TEMPERATURE.

SERVES 4–6

STUFFED CHICKEN
2½ cups jasmine rice
½ cup golden sultanas
1 red onion, sliced
5 cups chicken stock
50g butter
salt and freshly ground
    black pepper
1 size 18 free-range chicken,
    skin on, boneless (ask
    your butcher to de-bone)
100g pine nuts
zest of 2 lemons
½ cup roughly chopped
    Italian parsley
cooking string, for trussing
2 tbsp olive oil for rubbing
    chicken skin

EGGPLANT SALAD
4 eggplants, sliced into
    2cm rounds
1 tbsp dried oregano
50ml good-quality olive oil
seeds of 1 pomegranate
salt and freshly ground
    black pepper
2 punnets cherry tomatoes
2 tbsp fresh basil leaves

SALAD DRESSING
3 tbsp sherry vinegar
1 tbsp pomegranate molasses
1 tbsp good-quality olive oil

1. Preheat oven to 180°C.

2. Place rice, sultanas, onion, stock, butter, salt and freshly ground black pepper in an oven dish. Cover with tinfoil. Bake for approximately 45 minutes, until rice is cooked, then stir with a fork and allow to cool.

3. Lay chicken out on a board lengthways so that the breast is on the left and the thigh is on the right. Open tenderloins up so that chicken is flat. Overlap one thigh over the other thigh so there are no gaps in the chicken. Season with salt and freshly ground black pepper.

4. Lightly toast pine nuts by dry-roasting them in a frying pan for a few minutes, stirring regularly to avoid burning. Allow to cool slightly.

5. Once stuffing is cool, mix in lemon zest, parsley and cooled pine nuts. Check seasoning and adjust if necessary.

6. Spread stuffing in a horizontal log across the chicken, leaving enough space on either side to roll up. Roll up away from yourself, making sure you keep the thighs of the chicken overlapped while rolling. When complete, the seam should be on the bottom.

7. Using cooking string, tie up each end of the chicken and then tie in the middle. Rub skin with olive oil and season with salt.

8. Put chicken in a roasting tray and cook for 40–45 minutes until golden and the juices run clear.

9. Allow to rest, covered, for 10 minutes before slicing.

TO MAKE THE SALAD

1. Toss together eggplant, oregano, oil, pomegranate seeds, salt and freshly ground black pepper in a bowl.

2. Transfer to an oven tray and roast at 180°C for 15–20 minutes until golden.

3. For the dressing, lightly whisk vinegar, pomegranate molasses and oil together. When eggplant is cooked, toss with cherry tomatoes, basil and dressing. Serve straight away with the sliced chicken.

SLOW-COOKED PORK SHOULDER

—

IF YOU WANT TO COOK SOMETHING DIFFERENT FOR A SUNDAY ROAST, THIS IS IT. SERVE THE PORK
SHOULDER WHOLE IN ITS TRAY AT THE DINNER TABLE AND EVERYONE CAN PULL OFF A PIECE TO GO
WITH THEIR PARMESAN POLENTA.

SERVES 8

1.5kg free-range pork
    shoulder, skinless and
    boneless
salt and freshly ground
    black pepper
2 tbsp olive oil
1kg fennel bulbs, cut into
    quarters (reserve a
    handful of the green tips)
10 cloves garlic
rind of 5 oranges (use a
    peeler)
1½–2 litres milk
1 recipe Parmesan Polenta
    (see page 110), to serve

1. Preheat oven to 150°C.

2. Season pork generously with salt and freshly ground black
pepper.

3. In a large heavy-based saucepan, big enough to fit the whole
shoulder in, heat oil and brown pork until a dark golden colour on all
sides. This will take approximately 10 minutes on a medium to high
heat. Place pork in a roasting pan.

4. Remove excess fat from the browning saucepan. Lower heat
to medium. Add fennel quarters, garlic and orange rind and fry
on a low heat until golden. Scatter over pork in roasting pan.
Add fennel tips.

5. In the same saucepan, gently heat milk until hot to the touch
(do not let it boil).

6. Pour hot milk over pork so that it comes half to two-thirds
of the way up the side of the pork. Cover with tinfoil and cook
for 3–3¼ hours. The pork is cooked when there is no resistance
when you insert a knife into the meat.

7. To serve, use tongs to pull meat apart. Reserve the milk, some
of which will have formed into curds. Serve pork with the cooked
fennel and oranges and Parmesan Polenta (see page 110), with milk
and curds poured over.

PARMESAN POLENTA

—

YOU COULD SERVE ANYTHING YOU LIKE ON TOP OF THIS POLENTA – PAN-FRIED MUSHROOMS, ROASTED PUMPKIN, WILTED SPINACH. IT IS SUPER VERSATILE.

SERVES 8

2.2 litres water
salt and freshly ground black
   pepper
500g quick-cook corn
   polenta
100g unsalted butter
150g grated Parmesan

—

Cook's note: If you want an even richer version of this polenta, use milk instead of water. If you prefer a runnier polenta, just add more liquid; or if you prefer it thicker, reduce the amount of liquid used.

—

1. Bring water to the boil. Add a good pinch of salt.

2. While whisking slowly, pour polenta into boiling water. Reduce heat to low. Keep whisking till polenta starts to thicken. Be careful that the polenta does not splatter you as it starts to thicken.

3. Using a wooden spoon, stir thickened polenta for 3–5 minutes, or until it has lost its crunch and is smooth on the tongue.

4. Add butter and Parmesan and mix to combine. Check seasoning, adjusting if necessary, and remove from heat. Serve immediately.

ASIAN BRAISED BEEF CHEEKS

—

BEEF CHEEKS ARE A BEAUTIFUL, MOIST AND MEATY CUT OF BEEF AND ARE GOOD TO USE
IN ANY SLOW COOKING RECIPE. IF YOU HAVEN'T TRIED THEM BEFORE, GIVE THEM A GO
USING THIS RECIPE. IT'S DELICIOUS!

SERVES 6

STOCK
2 whole red chillies
1 bunch coriander
zest and juice of 2 oranges
500ml soy sauce
250ml rice wine vinegar
2cm piece ginger, unpeeled,
    roughly chopped
3 cinnamon sticks
4 star anise
3 litres water
1 whole bulb garlic, cut
    in half
300g fresh shiitake
    mushrooms
1½ cups brown sugar

BEEF
2 tbsp olive oil
6 whole beef cheeks,
    trimmed and sinew
    removed
salt and freshly ground
    black pepper

1. Preheat oven to 150°C.

2. Pierce chillies several times with the tip of a knife. Remove
leaves from coriander and reserve leaves for garnish. Using a potato
peeler, remove zest from oranges and then juice the oranges.

3. Place chillies, coriander stalks, orange zest and juice into a large
stockpot. Add remaining stock ingredients, except brown sugar.

4. Place pot over a medium heat and bring to a simmer, then remove
from heat and set aside while you cook the beef cheeks.

5. Heat oil in a large ovenproof casserole dish. Season beef cheeks
with salt and freshly ground black pepper, then brown cheeks in
the hot oil until nicely golden all over. (You may need to do this
in batches.)

6. Add brown sugar to stock and place over a medium heat. Stir
to dissolve sugar and simmer until the sauce starts to thicken.
Continue cooking to reduce sauce by a third (approximately
10–15 minutes).

7. Pour reduced sauce over beef cheeks in the casserole dish and
cover tightly with a lid or layer of tinfoil. Cook in preheated oven
for 3½–4 hours, until meat is meltingly tender.

8. Using tongs, remove the beef cheeks to a plate and pull meat
apart into large chunks. Return to the sauce.

9. Garnish with reserved coriander leaves. Delicious served with
steamed jasmine rice and bok choy.

DESSERT

—

It is so satisfying to complete a meal with a sensational sweet treat, whether it comes in the form of a pie laden with in-season fruit or a hot, rich chocolate pudding oozing with molten chocolate. To us, dessert is the most important part of dinner as it is the last item you eat and leaves a lasting impression. If you end a meal with a poor dessert it taints the whole meal.

To achieve a top pudding, don't skimp on ingredients. We only use really good-quality chocolate (at least 50% cocoa solids) and cocoa. The best flavour comes from organic fruit, so where possible choose organic over sprayed, and only buy in season.

There are two categories of desserts included here. One is your simple pud for a quick weeknight dessert which you can whip up in 30 minutes, such as the Sticky Date Pudding (see page 148) or the Creamy Rice Pudding (see page 120). Then there is the grand dessert, which will take time to create, like the Chocolate Ginger Mousse Cake (see page 128). You will most likely need to make some components a day ahead, but I guarantee it will be the showstopper finish to your dinner party.

APRICOT AND HAZELNUT TORTE

—

YOU CAN CHANGE THE FRUIT IN THIS CAKE TO PLUMS, WHICH ARE ALSO A GREAT MARRIAGE
WITH THE HAZELNUTS.

MAKES ONE 23CM TORTE

POACHED APRICOTS
16 apricots
1–2 cups sugar (depending
    on tartness of apricots)
zest and juice of 3 oranges

CAKE
125g unsalted butter,
    softened
¾ cup muscovado sugar
¼ tsp vanilla paste
zest of 4 oranges
2 large eggs
2 tbsp runny honey
½ cup ground hazelnuts or
    ground almonds
1 cup flour, sifted
2 tsp baking powder, sifted
4 tbsp yoghurt
¼ cup caster sugar

-

Cook's note: Leftover apricot syrup
can be served over ice cream. It
can also be frozen for later use.

-

1. Preheat oven to 150°C.

2. Cut apricots in half and remove stones. Lay cut-side down on
a baking dish.

3. Mix sugar, orange zest and juice in a bowl and pour over apricots.

4. Bake for 20–25 minutes or until tender. Remove from oven
and cool.

5. Turn oven up to 180°C. Line the sides and base of a 23cm
loose-bottomed round tin with baking paper.

6. Using an electric beater on high speed, cream butter and
muscovado sugar until light and fluffy. Add vanilla and orange
zest, and combine.

7. Reduce speed to medium and add eggs one at a time, ensuring
that the first is fully combined before adding the second. Add honey.

8. Scrape down the sides of the bowl with a spatula and continue
mixing for another minute.

9. Remove bowl from mixer. Sprinkle ground hazelnuts or almonds
and sifted flour and baking powder over the mix. Using a metal
spoon, fold through until just combined. Add yoghurt and fold
through until just combined.

10. Using a slotted spoon, lay poached apricots on a clean, dry cloth
to remove excess moisture. If you do not dry the apricots, the cake
will be too wet.

11. Sprinkle the base of the lined tin with caster sugar and arrange
the apricots face down on the sugar, overlapping to create a double
layer. Spoon cake mix over the apricots.

12. Bake on the middle rack of the oven for 45–50 minutes, until the
top of the cake springs back when lightly touched.

13. Remove from oven and allow to cool before turning out. Decorate
with extra fresh seasonal fruits if desired.

CREAMY RICE PUDDING

—

RICE PUDDING IS MY ALL-TIME FAVOURITE COMFORT FOOD. THIS IS A QUICK, DELICIOUS, CREAMY PUDDING THAT CAN ALSO BE SERVED AS A BREAKFAST. IF YOU ARE DAIRY-INTOLERANT, SWAP OUT THE CRÈME FRAÎCHE FOR COCONUT YOGHURT.

SERVES 6

1 cup medium-grain rice
720ml milk
¼ cup caster sugar
1 tsp vanilla paste
1 tsp freshly grated nutmeg
1 cinnamon stick
180ml coconut milk
180g crème fraîche
1 recipe Poached Plums
  (see page 166)

1. Put rice, milk, sugar, vanilla, nutmeg and cinnamon stick in a heavy-based saucepan and simmer over a low heat for 25–30 minutes, stirring occasionally at first and then more frequently as it thickens to prevent it catching on the bottom.

2. Add coconut milk and simmer for another 10 minutes, stirring constantly. Transfer to a bowl and leave to cool.

3. When cool, remove the cinnamon stick. Fold through the crème fraîche. Spoon into 6 ramekins or jars and leave to set in the refrigerator for a few hours or overnight.

4. To serve, spoon 2 Poached Plums on top of rice and drizzle plum juice over.

FIG TART

—

FIG, ORANGE ZEST AND BLACKBERRIES ARE A PERFECT MATCH TOPPED WITH HONEY. BE CAREFUL NOT TO COOK THE FIGS TOO MUCH AS THEY WILL LOSE THEIR BEAUTIFUL PINK COLOUR. THAT IS WHY I PAR-COOK THE TART WITHOUT THE FRUIT TO LIMIT THE TIME THEY ARE IN THE OVEN.

MAKES ONE 12CM X 36CM TART

PASTRY
2¾ cups flour
1 cup icing sugar
pinch of salt
¼ tsp ground cinnamon
250g cold unsalted butter, chopped
1 egg
1 tsp orange juice
½ tsp orange zest
vanilla essence or paste, to taste

FILLING
zest and juice of 2 oranges
1 recipe (2 cups) Frangipane (see page 161)
1 cup frozen blackberries
½ cup good-quality honey
20 fresh figs, halved
handful of fresh blackberries, to garnish
mascarpone or Greek-style yoghurt, to serve

—

Cook's note: Any leftover pastry can be wrapped in cling film and frozen.

—

1. Place flour, icing sugar, salt and cinnamon in a food processor and pulse in 2-second bursts to aerate and combine.

2. Add butter and pulse until mixture resembles light breadcrumbs.

3. Add egg, orange juice, zest and vanilla and pulse 10 times. The mixture should look dry and crumbly.

4. Turn mixture out onto a clean surface and gather it together, then gently shape into a ball. Wrap in cling film and refrigerate for 2 hours before using.

5. On a lightly floured bench, roll out pastry to 3mm thick. Line a 12cm x 36cm loose-bottomed tart tin with pastry, trimming to form a neat edge. Place in refrigerator to rest for at least 1 hour.

6. Preheat oven to 180°C. Place a baking tray on the bottom rack of the oven to heat.

7. To make the filling, mix orange zest and juice through Frangipane. Spread into the chilled pastry case and scatter with frozen blackberries.

8. Place filled tart on heated baking tray and bake for 15 minutes.

9. Meanwhile, gently melt honey in a saucepan. Toss figs through the honey so they are fully coated.

10. Remove tart from oven and arrange figs over the filling. Bake for a further 15 minutes, until pastry is golden.

11. Remove from oven and garnish with fresh blackberries.

12. Serve hot or cold with mascarpone or Greek-style yoghurt.

RASPBERRY AND LEMON CAKE

—

THIS IS A GLUTEN-FREE ITALIAN CAKE WHICH I HAVE AMPED UP WITH SOME RASPBERRIES. IT IS
ABSOLUTELY IRRESISTIBLE WITH ITS MOREISH ALMOND FLAVOUR AND KEEPS MOIST FOR DAYS.

MAKES ONE 18CM CAKE

160g butter, softened
¾ cup icing sugar, plus
   extra to dust
4 eggs, separated
1 tsp baking powder
2 cups ground almonds
4 tbsp lemon juice
zest of 4 lemons
pinch of salt
1 cup frozen raspberries
½ cup Lemon Curd
   (see page 161)
½ cup mascarpone
½ cup slivered almonds
icing sugar, to dust
1 punnet fresh raspberries
½ cup Raspberry Coulis,
   to serve (see page 164)
cream or yoghurt, to serve

1. Preheat oven to 180°C. Line an 18cm round cake tin with baking
paper.

2. Using an electric mixer, beat butter and icing sugar until light
and fluffy. Add egg yolks one at a time, ensuring that each is fully
combined before adding the next.

3. In a separate bowl, mix baking powder, ground almonds, and
lemon juice and zest. Add to butter mixture and mix to combine.

4. In another bowl, free of grease, whisk egg whites and salt with
an electric mixer until very stiff peaks form.

5. Gently fold egg white a third at a time through cake mixture with
a metal spoon until just combined.

6. Spread half the cake mixture into the prepared tin. Sprinkle over
half the frozen raspberries and top with remaining cake mixture.
Sprinkle over remaining frozen raspberries.

7. Bake for 20 minutes, then turn the tin around in the oven. Lower
heat to 160°C and bake for a further 15–20 minutes until cake is
golden and the top springs back to the touch.

8. Remove from oven and cool in the tin on a wire rack, before
turning out of the tin to cool further.

9. When cake is cool, cut in half horizontally with a sharp bread
knife.

10. Using a palette knife, spread half the Lemon Curd over the base,
followed by the mascarpone.

11. Replace the top half of the cake. Using the palette knife, spread
the remaining Lemon Curd around the sides of the cake.

12. Press slivered almonds around the sides of the cake to coat.
Heavily dust the top of the cake with icing sugar and decorate
with fresh raspberries.

13. Serve with Raspberry Coulis and cream or yoghurt.

CHOCOLATE GINGER MOUSSE CAKE

–

THIS CAKE IS NOT AN EVERYDAY CAKE – IT TAKES EFFORT TO PULL IT OFF, BUT IT'S A REAL SHOWSTOPPER. WHENEVER THIS CAKE MADE AN APPEARANCE IN THE LITTLE & FRIDAY DINNER SHOP, AFTER HOURS, IT WOULD DISAPPEAR PRETTY QUICKLY AND THERE WAS NEVER ANY LEFT AT THE END OF SERVICE.

MAKES ONE 18CM CAKE

CAKE
250g dark chocolate
    (55% cocoa solids)
5 eggs
2½ cups sugar
300ml canola oil
200g fresh ginger, peeled
    and grated
2 cups high-grade flour
1 cup high-quality
    Dutch cocoa
2 tsp baking powder
1 tsp vanilla essence
200g sour cream

MOUSSE FILLING
AND TOPPING
400g dark chocolate
    (55% cocoa solids)
200g butter
1 tbsp whisky (optional)
8 eggs, separated
4 tsp sugar
1 cup mascarpone
1 recipe Chocolate Ganache
    (see page 164), still warm

CHOCOLATE CURLS
250g compound chocolate

SPUN SUGAR
120ml water
1½ cups caster sugar

TO MAKE THE CAKE

1. Preheat oven to 150°C. Line the bases and sides of three 20cm cake tins with baking paper.

2. Melt chocolate in a double boiler or a heatproof bowl set over a saucepan of simmering water. Cool to room temperature.

3. Using an electric mixer on medium speed, beat eggs and sugar together until light and creamy. The mixture is ready when it falls from the beater in a wide ribbon that holds its form before dissolving.

4. With the mixer on low speed, slowly drizzle in canola oil and mix until combined.

5. Add melted chocolate and ginger to egg mixture and mix until combined.

6. Sift flour, cocoa and baking powder into the egg mixture, and fold through with a metal spoon or clean hand until just combined. Fold through vanilla and sour cream.

7. Divide evenly into the 3 tins. Bake for 20 minutes, then turn tins around in the oven and bake for another 15–20 minutes, or until the tops spring back when touched lightly. Leave to cool in the tins.

8. Turn out cakes by inverting the tins, then turning cakes upright.

TO MAKE THE MOUSSE FILLING

1. Melt chocolate and butter together in a double boiler or a heatproof bowl set over a saucepan of simmering water. Allow to cool slightly, then add whisky, if desired.

2. Using a whisk, mix in egg yolks one at a time, ensuring that each is well combined before adding the next.

3. In another bowl, free of grease, whisk egg whites until just before they reach the soft peak stage. Slowly add sugar and continue to whip until firm peaks form.

4. Add beaten egg white a third at a time to chocolate mixture, using a metal spoon to fold it gently through until just combined. Place in refrigerator to chill.

RECIPE CONTINUED ON FOLLOWING PAGES

TO ASSEMBLE

1. Line the sides of an 18cm round cake tin with a 150mm-wide sheet of acetate. (Acetate will help to create a neat edge.)

2. Stack the three cakes on top of each other and shave off the edges with a sharp bread knife, so that all have a flat, even edge and will fit neatly inside the 18cm lined tin. Dip knife into boiling water regularly to get a clean cut.

3. Place the first cake in the tin and spread with a third of the mousse mixture. Spread this with half of the mascarpone. Repeat with the next cake. Place the third cake on top and spread with the remaining mousse.

4. Refrigerate for at least 8 hours, until mousse and mascarpone are set.

5. To remove the cake from the tin, place a plate on top and turn the tin upside down. Remove tin and place a wooden board on top of cake, then turn over again so that cake is upright. Peel off the acetate. Using a hot palette knife, smooth the mousse and mascarpone so that the cake has smooth sides.

6. Make Chocolate Ganache following the recipe on page 164. Pour warm ganache over the top of the cake so that it drizzles down the sides.

TO MAKE CHOCOLATE CURLS

1. Melt compound chocolate in a double boiler or a heatproof bowl set over a saucepan of simmering water.

2. Pour melted chocolate onto a clean bench; stainless steel or marble is ideal – nothing textured. Use a spatula to spread chocolate out to a thickness of 1mm. Allow to partially set.

3. Using a long knife or a bench scraper, gently scrape over the chocolate, away from you, to form curls. Altering the angle of the blade will change the size and shape of the curls.

4. Gently place curls on top of cake.

TO MAKE SPUN SUGAR

1. First prepare your work area – you will need to work quickly once the sugar syrup is ready. Place two wooden spoons about a hand-span apart on the bench, with the handles sticking out over the edge. Weigh down the spoon ends with something heavy, such as a couple of cookbooks. You might like to place newspaper on the floor underneath, as it can get a little messy. Have a large, heatproof bowl of cold water ready to sit a hot saucepan in.

2. Combine water and sugar in a clean saucepan and stir until it is the consistency of wet sand.

3. Place on a medium to high heat. It is important not to stir the mixture from this point on. Allow it to come to the boil, and while cooking make sure to keep the sides of the saucepan clean of sugar crystals using a wet pastry brush. Continue to cook until mixture is a warm golden colour.

4. Remove from heat and immerse the saucepan in the bowl of cold water. Let sit for 30 seconds, or until the sugar syrup just starts to thicken around the sides. Do not let any water splash into the pot or you will need to start again.

5. Holding two forks together back to back, dip them into the sugar and then flick them back and forth over the wooden spoon handles to form strands. You will have to work fast as the caramel will set quickly.

6. Gently lift sugar strands off the spoon handles and place around the cake. Be careful not to over-handle the strands, or they will clump together. Spun sugar is best when used immediately. If you struggle with the technique, flakes of edible gold leaf also look great as a garnish.

CHERRY AND RASPBERRY PIE

—

THE CHERRY SEASON TENDS TO BE SHORT, BUT AS PRICES DROP I BUY UP LARGE, PIT THE CHERRIES AND FREEZE THEM SO I CAN MAKE THIS DELICIOUS PIE THROUGHOUT SUMMER.

MAKES ONE 24CM PIE

1 recipe Sweet Pastry
   (see page 158)

FILLING

2kg fresh cherries, pitted
1 cup caster sugar
½ cup ground almonds
¼ cup cornflour
seeds of 1 vanilla bean
   (or ½ tsp vanilla paste)
zest of 1 lemon
zest of 4 oranges
2 punnets raspberries

TO FINISH

1 egg
1 tbsp cream
2 tbsp demerara sugar
whipped cream, to serve

1. Preheat oven to 180°C. Line the base and sides of a 24cm loose-bottomed tart tin with baking paper.

2. On a lightly floured bench, divide pastry in two. Roll both pastry sheets out to 5mm thick and use one sheet to line the bottom and sides of the prepared tin. Place the remaining pastry sheet on a tray. Chill lined tin and pre-rolled pastry sheet for 20 minutes in the refrigerator.

3. In a large bowl, combine all filling ingredients.

4. Spoon filling into the chilled pastry shell in a mound, so there is more filling in the centre. Do not fill higher than 1cm below the rim of the pie, or the filling will bubble over and make it difficult to remove the pie from the tin when cool.

5. Cut rolled-out pastry sheet into strips 15mm wide and 25mm long.

6. To make a simple lattice, lay a pastry strip vertically across the left edge of the pie. Place another strip horizontally across the top edge of the first strip. Continue across the pie, alternating between vertical and horizontal strips to create a lattice pattern. Trim the edges.

7. To make egg wash, place egg and cream in a bowl and whisk until smooth.

8. Brush lattice with egg wash and sprinkle with demerara sugar.

9. Bake until golden and cooked through, approximately 1 hour. A good indication of when it is ready is when the cherry mixture starts bubbling through the lattice.

10. Cool to room temperature. Chilling in the refrigerator will make it easier to cut, otherwise it may crumble. Serve hot or cold with whipped cream.

BANOFFEE PIE

—

BANOFFEE PIE IS AN OLD-FASHIONED ENGLISH DESSERT. AT THE CAFÉ, WE USE A COMBINATION OF ANY LEFTOVER BISCUITS TO CREATE THE CASE. THEY CAN CONTAIN CHOCOLATE, COCONUT OR NUTS – IT ALL WORKS AS THE FLAVOUR COMBINATION IS VERY ADAPTABLE.

MAKES ONE 28CM PIE

BASE
2 x 225g packets chocolate
  chip biscuits
½ cup good-quality Dutch
  cocoa
⅔ cup flour
½ cup ground almonds
pinch of salt
110g butter, melted

FILLING
1 recipe Chocolate Ganache
  (see page 164)
10 small or 5 large bananas
squeeze of lemon juice
250g unsalted butter
¾ cup firmly packed soft
  brown sugar
2 x 380g cans caramel
  dessert filling
pinch of salt

TOPPING
1 double espresso coffee
  shot, cooled
2½ cups mascarpone
2 tbsp good-quality Dutch
  cocoa

TO MAKE THE PIE CASE

1. Preheat oven to 180°C. Line a 28cm round springform tin with baking paper.

2. Using a kitchen whizz, blend biscuits to a breadcrumb-like texture. You will need 2 cups of crumbs.

3. In a bowl, combine biscuit crumbs with the other dry ingredients, then mix in melted butter.

4. Press mixture into the base and sides of the prepared tin until firm. Cover with baking paper and fill with blind-baking weights, ensuring that the weights fill the case to 1cm below the rim (or the case will shrink and crack).

5. Bake pie case for 15 minutes, then remove weights and baking paper and cook for a further 5–10 minutes. The case will still be slightly soft when you take it out of the oven, but the edges should be crisp. If base has bubbled, press it back down flat with a clean tea towel while still hot. Allow to cool.

TO MAKE THE FILLING

1. Once pie case is cool, spread Chocolate Ganache over base and sides.

2. Cut bananas in half lengthways and toss through lemon juice. Lay bananas over the ganache in a spiral, starting from the outside edge and working in. You will need to cut some of the bananas to fit as you get towards the centre, and should end up with two layers.

3. Melt butter and sugar together in a saucepan until sugar is dissolved.

4. In another saucepan, heat caramel dessert filling, stirring until smooth, then add to butter and sugar mixture. Add salt and bring to the boil, stirring until smooth. Remove from heat and allow to cool for 10 minutes before pouring into prepared pie case.

TO MAKE THE TOPPING

Fold espresso shot through mascarpone. Pipe over cooled pie, using an 18mm tip to create peaks. Dust with cocoa before serving.

STRAWBERRY AND RHUBARB CHEESECAKE

—

WE FIND IT IS BEST TO MAKE THIS DESSERT THE DAY BEFORE AND ALLOW IT TO CHILL IN
THE FRIDGE OVERNIGHT, AS IT IS MUCH EASIER TO CUT WHEN FIRM.

**MAKES ONE 23CM
CHEESECAKE**

1 recipe Sweet Pastry
(see page 158)

FILLING
1.5kg full-fat cream cheese
(I use Philadelphia)
1 cup sugar
3 eggs
5 egg yolks
200ml cream
zest of 3 lemons
seeds of 1 vanilla pod,
or 1 tsp vanilla paste

TOPPING
3 stalks rhubarb
zest and juice of 2 oranges
1 tsp rosewater
1 cup caster sugar
1 punnet strawberries

SAUCE
2 punnets strawberries
½ cup caster sugar
2 tbsp lemon juice
½ cup strawberry jam

1. Make Sweet Pastry following recipe on page 158.

2. Preheat oven to 180°C. Line the base and sides of a 23cm round
springform tin with baking paper.

3. On a lightly floured bench, roll out the pastry to 5mm thick. Line
the base and sides of the tin, allowing the top to overhang 1cm
around the edges. Chill in the refrigerator for 20 minutes.

4. Cover pastry with baking paper and fill with blind-baking weights,
ensuring that the weights fill the case to 1cm below the rim or it will
shrink and crack. Bake for 20 minutes.

5. Remove blind-baking weights and paper, turn oven down to 150°C
and bake pastry shell for another 20 minutes. Remove from oven
(leaving oven on) and allow to cool.

6. Using a sharp knife, shave off the overhanging edges of pastry.
Cut away from the centre rather than inwards, or the pastry will
collapse.

TO MAKE THE FILLING
1. Place cream cheese in the bowl of a food processor and blend
until smooth. Add sugar and blend for a few more minutes until fully
combined. You may need to do this in two batches, depending on the
size of your food processor.

2. Add whole eggs one at a time, followed by the yolks also one at a
time. Add cream, lemon zest and vanilla and blend until combined.

3. Pour mixture into the cooled pastry shell and bake for 40 minutes.
Turn oven down to 130°C and bake for another 20 minutes.

4. Allow cheesecake to cool completely in tin before placing in
refrigerator to set for a few hours. When fully chilled, remove
from the tin.

TO MAKE THE TOPPING

1. Preheat oven to 180°C.

2. Cut rhubarb into 8cm-long pieces and place in a baking dish.

3. In a bowl, combine orange zest and juice, rosewater and ½ cup sugar. Pour over rhubarb and toss to coat.

4. Bake for approximately 20–30 minutes or until tender, turning rhubarb occasionally. Remove from oven and allow to cool.

5. Halve strawberries and place cut-side down on a tray. Sprinkle with remaining ½ cup sugar and leave to sit for 20 minutes.

6. Toss strawberries and cooled rhubarb together and pile on top of cheesecake.

7. To make the sauce, halve the strawberries and place in a medium saucepan. Add sugar and lemon juice and gently boil for 2 minutes.

8. Add strawberry jam and cook for another minute, stirring until combined. Sieve or use a food processor to create a smooth sauce.

9. Drizzle sauce over garnished cheesecake, reserving some to drizzle over cut slices.

10. Chill in the refrigerator and when ready to serve, slice with a sharp knife. Dip knife into hot water regularly to get a clean cut.

SEE PHOTO ON PAGE 140

MANGO TART

—

IT MAY SEEM A LOT OF WORK TO MAKE ALL THE COMPONENTS TO THIS TART, BUT IT IS WELL WORTH THE EFFORT. I SUGGEST YOU MAKE A DOUBLE RECIPE OF PASTRY TO LINE TWO TINS. YOU WILL THEN HAVE AN EXTRA TART CASE THAT YOU CAN FREEZE AND PULL OUT ON THE DAY IT'S REQUIRED. DO NOT THAW THE PASTRY BUT FILL AND COOK IT WHILE FROZEN.

MAKES ONE 12CM X 36CM TART

1 recipe Sweet Pastry (see page 158)
½ recipe (1 cup) Frangipane (see page 161)
1 cup Crème Pâtissière (see page 160)
1 cup frozen raspberries
3 fresh ripe mangoes
1 cup Crème Diplomat (see page 160)
1 tbsp icing sugar
handful of fresh raspberries, to decorate (optional)

1. On a lightly floured bench, roll out pastry to 3mm thick and use to line a 12cm x 36cm loose-bottomed tart tin, trimming pastry to form a neat edge. Place in refrigerator to rest for at least 1 hour.

2. Preheat oven to 180°C. Place a baking tray on the bottom rack of the oven to heat.

3. Spread Frangipane into chilled pastry case, then fill to just below the rim with Crème Pâtissière. Sprinkle frozen raspberries over.

4. Place tart on heated tray in oven and bake until pastry is golden, approximately 30 minutes depending on your oven.

5. Peel mangoes and slice lengthways as thinly as you can.

6. When tart is cooked, remove from oven and allow to cool completely. Cover the top with Crème Diplomat and dust with icing sugar.

7. Lay slices of mango on top of the tart in a spiral pattern, starting from the inside and working out to the edges to form a flower design. You should fit four spirals the length of the tart. Scatter fresh raspberries over if desired.

8. Serve cold with any remaining Crème Diplomat. This tart is best eaten the same day.

CHOCOLATE HAZELNUT BISCUITS

—

KEEP THESE BISCUITS IN AN AIRTIGHT JAR READY FOR A SUPER EASY, GLUTEN-FREE,
IMPROMPTU DESSERT. JUST ADD YOUR FAVOURITE ICE CREAM!

MAKES 12

2¼ cups icing sugar
½ cup good-quality
   Dutch cocoa
pinch of salt
½ cup chocolate chips
1 cup roasted whole
   hazelnuts (see Cook's
   note)
3 egg whites
1 tsp vanilla essence
ice cream, to serve

—

Cook's note: To roast the
hazelnuts, place on a lined baking
tray and roast for 10 minutes in
a 140°C oven.

—

1. Preheat oven to 160°C. Line a baking tray with baking paper.

2. Combine icing sugar, cocoa, salt, chocolate chips and roasted hazelnuts in a large bowl.

3. Mix egg whites and vanilla together, add to the chocolate mixture and mix well. This will create quite a wet, sticky mixture.

4. Scoop tablespoons of mixture onto prepared baking tray, spacing them 5cm apart.

5. Leave tray out at room temperature for 20 minutes until biscuit mixture dries out slightly, forming a skin on the surface. (This is a very wet mix.)

6. Bake for 15 minutes. Allow to cool on tray.

7. Sandwich together with your favourite ice cream!

STICKY DATE PUDDING

—

I'M SURE MANY PEOPLE WILL REMEMBER THIS DESSERT FONDLY FROM THEIR CHILDHOOD. THIS RECIPE IS FAIL-SAFE AND ALWAYS COMES OUT MOIST AND FULL OF FLAVOUR. SERVE THE PUDDING STEAMING HOT WITH POURING CREAM OR A GOOD-QUALITY ICE CREAM.

SERVES 10

PUDDING
4½ cups chopped dried dates
450ml water
2 tsp baking soda
180g butter
1½ cups soft brown sugar, firmly packed
½ tsp vanilla paste
5 eggs
2½ cups self-raising flour

CARAMEL SAUCE
2 cups caster sugar
600ml cream

TO SERVE
fresh dates, halved, for decoration
mascarpone or vanilla ice cream

TO MAKE THE PUDDING
1. Preheat oven to 180°C. Line a 25cm x 30cm baking dish with baking paper.

2. Place chopped dates and water in a saucepan and bring to the boil. Remove from heat and stir in baking soda. Allow to sit for 15 minutes.

3. Cream butter, brown sugar and vanilla in an electric mixer on a medium speed until pale and fluffy.

4. Add eggs one at a time, making sure each is fully combined before adding the next.

5. Sift flour and fold into butter mixture, being careful not to over-mix. Fold through the cooled date paste.

6. Spoon into prepared dish and bake for 20 minutes, then turn dish around in the oven and bake for another 15–20 minutes, until the top of the pudding bounces back when lightly pressed.

TO MAKE THE SAUCE
1. Place caster sugar in a small saucepan and just cover with water until it is the consistency of wet sand.

2. Bring to the boil but do not stir. Use a wet pastry brush to clean down the sides of the saucepan to remove any stray sugar crystals.

3. Continue to boil until sugar turns amber. At this point, quickly remove from heat.

4. In a separate small saucepan, heat cream to boiling point. Gradually add cream to the caramelised sugar, stirring constantly to achieve a smooth consistency.

TO SERVE
Cut pudding into squares while still hot and pour over hot caramel sauce. Top with fresh date halves. Serve with mascarpone or vanilla ice cream.

PEAR AND HAZELNUT LAYER CAKE

—

HAZELNUT MERINGUE IS LAYERED WITH HAZELNUT SPREAD IN THIS DECADENT CAKE, WHICH MAKES A GOOD WINTER DESSERT WHEN FRUIT OPTIONS ARE LIMITED. YOU CAN ASSEMBLE THIS THE DAY BEFORE AND STORE OVERNIGHT IN THE FRIDGE TO SLIGHTLY SOFTEN THE MERINGUE, WHICH WILL MAKE CUTTING IT A LITTLE EASIER.

MAKES ONE 20CM CAKE

MERINGUE
9 egg whites
1½ cups sugar
5 cups ground hazelnuts
½ tsp salt
½ tsp vanilla paste

HONEYED PEARS
12 pears, skin on
1 cup good-quality honey
1 tsp vanilla paste
100g butter

HAZELNUT SPREAD
2 cups whole hazelnuts,
    skin on
120g butter
450g dark chocolate
    (55% cocoa solids)
¼ cup sugar
1 cup cream
pinch of salt

TO FINISH
2 cups mascarpone

TO MAKE MERINGUE

1. Preheat oven to 150°C. Line three baking trays with baking paper. Draw a 20cm circle on each piece of baking paper (you can trace around a 20cm cake tin).

2. Place egg whites in a clean, dry mixing bowl and whisk with an electric beater on high speed until soft peaks form. Gradually add sugar, continuing to beat until fully combined and meringue mixture is glossy.

3. Using a metal spoon, fold through ground hazelnuts, salt and vanilla paste, being careful not to over-mix.

4. Spoon a third of the mixture in the centre of the circle on each tray and spread out to a flat disk, using your drawn circles as a guide.

5. Bake for 40 minutes, then turn oven down to 140°C and bake for a further 20 minutes. Cool on wire racks before removing meringue from baking paper.

TO MAKE HONEYED PEARS

1. Preheat oven to 200°C.

2. Halve 3 pears and quarter the rest. Core all of the pear pieces.

3. In a small saucepan, melt honey, vanilla and butter over a low heat.

4. Place pear pieces in a baking dish and pour over honey mixture, making sure pears are fully coated.

5. Bake for 20 minutes, then remove from oven and baste with the honey mixture in the dish. Turn oven down to 180°C and cook for a further 20 minutes, basting again after 10 minutes. Cool in the dish.

RECIPE CONTINUED ON FOLLOWING PAGES

TO MAKE HAZELNUT SPREAD

1. Preheat oven to 140°C. Line a baking tray with baking paper.

2. Place hazelnuts on lined baking tray and roast for 10 minutes.

3. Melt butter and chocolate in a small saucepan over a low heat and allow to cool.

4. Remove hazelnuts from oven and rub them between the folds of a clean tea towel to remove skins.

5. Place nuts in a food processor with sugar and blitz until fine crumbs form.

6. Pour in melted chocolate mixture and cream, add salt and blitz until fully combined. Refrigerate until ready to use.

TO ASSEMBLE

1. Spread hazelnut spread evenly over meringue discs.

2. Spread 2 meringues with mascarpone and top with the quartered honeyed pears. Stack these 2 meringues on top of each other. Finish with the third meringue disc, with the hazelnut spread facing up.

3. Arrange the honeyed pear halves on top, to decorate.

SELF-SAUCING CHOCOLATE PUDDINGS

—

THIS IS CHOCOLATE HEAVEN, WITH A GOOEY, SOFT CHOCOLATE CENTRE SO PERFECT FOR
A COLD WINTER'S NIGHT. SERVE WITH FRESH CREAM OR A TOP-QUALITY VANILLA ICE CREAM.

SERVES 6

1 cup self-raising flour
3 tbsp good-quality
   Dutch cocoa
½ cup firmly packed soft
   brown sugar
80g butter, melted
1 egg
½ cup milk

SAUCE
¾ cup firmly packed soft
   brown sugar
2 tbsp good-quality
   Dutch cocoa
1 cup boiling water

GARNISH
100g good-quality milk
   chocolate, roughly
   chopped

1. Preheat oven to 180°C. Line a baking dish with baking paper.

2. Grease 6 ovenproof mugs or ramekins, each approximately 300ml capacity.

3. Sift flour and cocoa into a large bowl and stir in sugar.

4. Place melted butter, egg and milk in a separate bowl and whisk to combine.

5. Slowly add egg mixture to flour mixture, whisking until smooth. Spoon evenly into mugs or ramekins.

6. For the sauce, combine sugar and cocoa and sprinkle evenly over the puddings.

7. Slowly pour boiling water over the back of a large metal spoon to evenly cover each pudding.

8. Place mugs or ramekins on prepared baking dish. Bake for 20–30 minutes, or until puddings bounce back when pressed gently in the centre.

9. Garnish with chunks of milk chocolate.

BASICS

—

SWEET PASTRY

—

MAKES ONE TART CASE

2¾ cups flour
1 cup icing sugar
pinch of salt
250g unsalted butter, cubed
1 egg
1 tsp lemon juice
½ tsp lemon zest
vanilla extract or paste, to taste

1. In a food processor, combine flour, icing sugar and salt and pulse in 2-second bursts to aerate and combine.

2. Add butter and pulse until mixture resembles breadcrumbs.

3. Add egg, lemon juice, zest and vanilla and pulse 10 times. The mixture should look dry and crumbly.

4. Turn out onto a clean bench and gather mixture together with your hands. Gently shape mixture into a ball.

5. Wrap in cling film and refrigerate for 2 hours before using.

FLAKY PASTRY

—

MAKES ONE 30CM X 40CM SHEET

3 cups flour
pinch of salt
450g unsalted butter, frozen
180ml iced water

1. Sift flour and salt into a large bowl. Grate 180g butter into bowl and, using your fingertips, work it into flour.

2. Dice remaining butter into 1cm cubes and add to bowl. Lightly mix with your hands until butter cubes are coated with flour mixture.

3. Add iced water and mix with your hands until dough starts to come together. The mixture will be studded with large lumps of butter and will be quite dry at this point.

4. Tip mixture onto a lightly floured bench and gently work together with your hands to form a rough ball.

5. Roll out to a 30cm x 20cm rectangle. With the long side facing you, fold the short sides in to meet at the centre. Fold in half to form a square.

6. Wrap in cling film and chill in refrigerator for at least 2 hours, or ideally overnight.

7. Roll into a 30cm x 20cm rectangle and fold as before. Do this twice, then return the pastry to the refrigerator for 30 minutes to rest.

8. On a lightly floured bench, roll pastry out to a 30cm x 40cm sheet, 6mm thick. Best used within 24 hours.

—

Cook's note: Pastry must be kept cool, so no hot hands or equipment. The longer you leave your pastry to rest in the refrigerator between rolls and folds, the flakier it will be.

—

CRÈME PÂTISSIÈRE
—

MAKES 2½ CUPS

500ml milk
1 tsp vanilla essence or paste
½ cup caster sugar
3 egg yolks
¼ cup cornflour

1. In a saucepan, combine milk, vanilla and half the caster sugar and bring to the boil.

2. In a separate bowl beat together remaining caster sugar, egg yolks and cornflour until pale and thick.

3. Slowly pour half the milk mixture into the egg mixture, whisking constantly. Return remaining milk mixture to the heat. When it has reached boiling point, quickly add the egg mixture, whisking constantly. As you add the egg mixture to the milk it will cool slightly. Keep whisking combined mixture vigorously over a medium heat until it returns to the boil, then remove from heat.

4. Pour into a bowl and lay a circle of baking paper on top so it does not form a film on the surface.

—

Cook's note: Crème pâtissière will keep in an airtight container in the refrigerator for up to 3 days. Beat until smooth before using, as it will form a solid mass once chilled.

—

CRÈME DIPLOMAT
—

MAKES 2½ CUPS

150ml cream
½ recipe Crème Pâtissière
    (see left), chilled

1. Whip cream until firm peaks form.

2. Beat chilled Crème Pâtissière until smooth. Fold gently through whipped cream using a metal spoon. Refrigerate in an airtight container for up to 3 days.

FRANGIPANE

—

MAKES 2 CUPS

125g unsalted butter, softened
½ cup caster sugar
2 eggs
1½ cups ground almonds
1 tbsp flour

1. Cream butter and sugar with an electric mixer until light and fluffy. Stop the beater and scrape down the sides of the bowl frequently to ensure that ingredients are being thoroughly combined.

2. Add eggs one at a time and beat well. Ensure that the first egg is fully combined before adding the next.

3. Using a wooden spoon, stir in ground almonds and flour to form a paste.

4. Refrigerate in an airtight container. Will keep for up to 2 weeks.

LEMON CURD

—

MAKES 2 CUPS

125g unsalted butter
1 cup caster sugar
zest and juice of 4 lemons
3 large eggs

1. Place all ingredients except eggs in a metal bowl. Place bowl over a saucepan of simmering water and stir until sugar has dissolved completely. You can check this by rubbing a small amount of cooled mixture between your fingers. It is not ready if the consistency is still granular.

2. Remove from heat. In a separate large metal bowl, whisk the eggs by hand to just combine. Add butter and sugar mixture to egg and beat until combined.

3. Pour mixture through a strainer into a clean metal bowl, to remove zest.

4. Place bowl back over simmering water and cook slowly until thick enough to coat the back of a spoon.

5. Cool and store in an airtight container in the refrigerator for up to 3 weeks.

RASPBERRY COULIS

—

CHOCOLATE GANACHE

—

MAKES 2½ CUPS

4 cups raspberries, fresh or frozen
¼ cup caster sugar
¾ cup water
juice of 1 lemon
2 tbsp cornflour
2 tbsp water

1. Place raspberries in a large saucepan. Add sugar, water and lemon juice and bring to a simmer.

2. Blend cornflour with 2 tbsp water to make a smooth paste and add to berry mixture.

3. Bring mixture to the boil, stirring constantly to prevent it catching on the bottom. Cook for 5 minutes. Cool. Will keep refrigerated in an airtight container for up to 4 weeks.

—

Cook's note: This mixture can also be blended to make a purée. However, we prefer to keep the fruit chunky to add texture to our donuts, cakes and meringues.

—

MAKES 1 CUP

200g dark chocolate (55% cocoa solids)
½ cup cream

1. Gently melt chocolate and cream in a double boiler or a heatproof bowl set over a saucepan of simmering water. Stir constantly to form a smooth sauce.

2. Allow to cool and thicken before using.

POACHED PEARS

—

MAKES 6

2 star anise
2 cinnamon sticks
1 tbsp manuka honey
1 cup caster sugar
6 pears, peeled and cored

1. Cut a circle of baking paper to fit the circumference of a saucepan large enough to hold all the pears. Cut a hole in the centre of the circle to let steam out. This will be used as a cartouche to prevent the pears discolouring.

2. Place enough water in saucepan to cover pears and bring to the boil.

3. Add spices, honey and caster sugar to pan. Stir until sugar has dissolved, then add pears.

4. Place the cartouche on the surface of the water. Simmer pears for 30 minutes, or until they have softened and become transparent but are still holding their shape. Every so often, carefully press down on the cartouche to release any steam.

5. Remove pears and syrup from pan and allow to cool before using. Pears can be refrigerated in an airtight container in their syrup for up to 5 days.

POACHED PLUMS

—

SERVES 6

12 plums
juice of 2 lemons
300ml water
¼ cup caster sugar

1. Cut plums in half and remove stones.

2. Place 12 plum halves in a blender with lemon juice and water and purée until very smooth. Add sugar and blend briefly to combine, then pour into a small saucepan.

3. Add remaining plum halves and simmer on a low heat until plums are tender, about 15 minutes. They will keep in an airtight container in the refrigerator for up to 5 days.

CANDIED WALNUTS

—

CANDIED HAZELNUTS

—

MAKES 500G

500g walnut pieces
150g good-quality runny honey

1. Preheat oven to 140°C. Line a baking tray with baking paper.

2. In a bowl, combine walnuts and honey and mix well. Spread out in a single layer on prepared tray.

3. Bake for 25–30 minutes, stirring every 5 minutes, or until walnuts are golden brown and glossy.

4. Remove from oven and cool. Stored in an airtight container, these will keep for 3–4 weeks.

—

Cook's note: These are great to have in the cupboard to sprinkle on porridge, ice cream or iced cakes.

—

MAKES 1 CUP

150g hazelnuts, skin on
75g good-quality runny honey

1. Preheat oven to 140°C. Line a baking tray with baking paper.

2. In a bowl, combine hazelnuts and honey and mix well. Spread out in a single layer on prepared tray.

3. Bake for 20–25 minutes, stirring every 5 minutes, or until hazelnuts are golden brown and glossy.

4. Remove from oven and cool. Stored in an airtight container, these will last for 1–2 weeks.

STEVE RICKERBY, OUR COMPOST GUY

WHIPPED BUTTER

—

HAZELNUT BUTTER

—

MAKES 450G

1 litre cream
1 tsp flaky sea salt, or to taste

1. Using an electric mixer with a whisk attachment, whisk cream on high speed until it becomes a solid mass, leaving a milky whey (approximately 10 minutes). The cream will thicken and then go lumpy before starting to separate.

2. Reduce mixer speed to medium to prevent whey splashing over edge of bowl. Butter will start to develop a crumble-like consistency. Keep whisking until it comes together into a ball. Drain whey from bowl.

3. Squeeze butter with your hands to remove excess liquid, then rinse under cold water. This washes the butter and removes any impurities, and will help the butter last longer.

4. Return butter to the bowl and add salt. Using a paddle attachment, mix on high speed for about 5 minutes or until white and fluffy.

5. Refrigerate in an airtight container. Will keep for 3–4 weeks.

MAKES 550G

100g hazelnuts
1 recipe Whipped Butter (see left), at room
    temperature
1 tbsp good-quality cocoa

1. Preheat oven to 180°C.

2. Place hazelnuts on a baking tray and roast for 10 minutes. When cool, rub nuts between folds of a tea towel to remove skins. Chop hazelnuts roughly.

3. Place butter in a bowl and fold through the hazelnuts and cocoa. Don't fully combine, as you want to create a ripple effect. Refrigerate in an airtight container. Will keep for 3–4 weeks.

ONION JAM

—

MAKES 1 CUP

2 tbsp extra virgin olive oil
3 cloves garlic, chopped
50g unsalted butter
¼ cup brown sugar
¼ cup balsamic vinegar
4 red onions, sliced
2 tbsp chopped thyme leaves
salt and freshly ground pepper

1. In a heavy-based saucepan, heat the olive oil over a medium heat and cook the garlic for a couple of minutes, but do not brown. Add butter, sugar and vinegar and combine before adding onions and thyme.

2. Turn heat to low and cook for approximately 25 minutes, stirring frequently to prevent mixture sticking to the bottom of the pan. Season with salt and pepper.

3. Cool before spooning into an airtight container. Onion Jam will keep for up to two weeks in an airtight container in the refrigerator.

RASPBERRY AND FIG JAM

—

MAKES 8 X 250ML JARS

1kg frozen raspberries
500g fresh figs, chopped
8 green apples, peeled, cored and
    diced (reserve peel and cores)
1.5kg white sugar
⅓ cup lemon juice

1. Put a plate in the freezer to chill.

2. Place raspberries, figs and diced apples in a large heavy-based saucepan and place over a medium heat. Cook for 5 minutes to soften, then add sugar and increase the heat, stirring gently until sugar dissolves and mixture begins to boil. Do not stir once mixture is boiling. Reduce heat and simmer for 15 minutes.

3. Using a slotted spoon remove fruit pulp to a large bowl. Add reserved apple peel and cores and lemon juice to jam mixture and continue cooking gently for 10–15 minutes.

4. Remove apple peel and cores with a slotted spoon and return fruit pulp to the jam mixture. Stir to combine.

5. Remove the chilled plate from the freezer and drop a spoonful of jam onto it. Place the plate in the freezer for a few minutes then nudge the jam with your finger. If a crust has formed and it wrinkles, it is ready. If not, continue cooking for another 10 minutes, and re-test in the same way.

6. Spoon cooked jam immediately into sterilised jars and seal. (You can sterilise jars by placing them on a clean baking tray in an oven preheated to 150°C for 10 minutes.) Turn filled jars upside down for 2 minutes to ensure lids have sealed properly. Set jars upright and store for up to 6 months in a cool, dry place.

INDEX

—

HELPFUL HINTS

—

CHOCOLATE

For baking we use a minimum of 50% cocoa solids, nothing less, as it will definitely alter the flavour. Compound chocolate is a substitute product made from cocoa, sweeteners and vegetable fat, which is easier to melt and work with. We use it for chocolate decorations.

EGGS

We use size 7 eggs for baking and I highly recommend free-range eggs. Not only are they more ethical, they have much better flavour. Make sure you bring eggs to room temperature before using.

FLOUR

Unless otherwise stated, the recipes in this book use plain or standard flour. For breads and doughs, we use high-grade flour. It is higher in protein (gluten), which strengthens the dough. Tipo 00 flour is an Italian flour used for pasta making. It gives the dough a silky texture and holds the pasta together while cooking.

SUGAR

We use caster sugar in all our baking because it dissolves more quickly and easily than regular white sugar.

YEAST

We generally prefer to use fresh yeast, which is available from specialty food stores. If you can't find it, you can use instant dry yeast instead.

OVEN KNOW-HOW

The temperatures used in this book are for fan-bake unless otherwise stated. If your oven only has regular bake you may need to increase the oven temperature by 20°C. All ovens are different, especially older models, so check baked items 10 minutes before the recommended cooking time.

This book would not have been possible without the help of so many talented team members at Little & Friday. From the many creatives who collaborated to put these ideas together, to the dishwasher who cleaned up after us daily while we played around with the ideas that finally became pages in this book.

A special thanks to Sophie Beck, my right hand lady, whose continual dedication and committed hard work (like no other) has allowed Little & Friday to move forward with new ideas and directions which are reflected in this book.

Thank you to Elizabeth Birch, Kate Bedford, Hannah Sosich, Eli Munro, Lisa Pijper, Sam Choi, Stephen Comans and Maros Vanovec for your assistance in developing these recipes. Thanks too to the Little & Friday team who kept the ball rolling while Sophie and I were consumed in photography shoots and brainstorming sessions.

I am very grateful to Debra Millar at Penguin Random House – this is our third book together and it gets easier every time. Thank you for continually believing in our vision and backing Little & Friday for all these years. To Debra's team, it is so nice to work with people that absolutely get what we are about, and together we have produced the best yet.

A very big thank you to Lottie Hedley and Holly Houston, the photographic and styling duo. Each shot in this book is so beautiful and together you have created a cohesive body of images that make the food jump off the pages. Thanks also to Lianne of The Props Department for her support, and to Holly for the ceramics.

I would also like to thank all those who supply Little & Friday with amazing produce on a daily basis. It is crucial for our success to be aligned with other companies that have the same attention to detail and passion for their product; The Art of Produce, The Produce Company, Fresh As, The Casual Foodie, Otaika Valley Free Range Eggs, Coffee Supreme, Northern Milk Supplies, Clevedon Valley Buffalo Company, Curious Croppers, Equagold, Heilala Vanilla, A Cracker of a Nut, Karma Cola, All Good Organics, The Secret Garden, Innocent Packaging, Westmere Butchery, Jerschke Honey, Fine & Dandy Tea, Davis Trading and Euro Dell.

My family also deserves a mention as for seven years now this business has been all-consuming for me. Holly Houston and Izaak Houston, both of you have enabled me to fulfil my dream, thank you. Chris Smart, thank you for being incredibly smart and having such an analytical brain and for giving me a granddaughter. Willow Smart, thank you for being so delicious – you are the only person who can make me stop work to play! You as a family have been so very valuable to this business.

Last but not least, thank you to all the Little & Friday customers who loyally come in and support us on our good days and also on our difficult ones. It has been a great joy to cook for you and to see the enjoyment you all received from our food over the last seven years.

KIM

My deepest appreciation to Kim, who gave me the opportunity to co-write this book with her. Her sheer determination and belief in what she does is an absolute inspiration. My gratitude also to the outstanding team I have behind me at Little & Friday. Their commitment and enthusiasm is the foundation for success in all that we do.

Thank you to my partner, Peter, who has supported me through the many hours I have spent at work over the years, allowing me to develop into the chef I have become today.

To my family, Mum, Dad, Chris, Tim and Sarah, my role models in so many different aspects of life. I wouldn't be the person I am today without you. Thank you.

SOPHIE